Many blessings
on the beautiful
journey ahead!

Brandi

Signed by the Author

RAISINGABLESSING.COM

Praise for *A Time to Dance: Chasing Joy in Difficult Seasons*

Grab your cup of coffee (or tea), a pen, and journal, and be ready to write down gems like this one: "Joy. It is not a season or an emotion. It's a process of placing our heart in God's loving hands, anchoring our hope and peace to His promises, accepting His truth about our identity, and faithfully submitting our life to His guidance and protection."

The author starts her story broken on the bathroom floor. My story started in the same way, only mine was on the closet floor. Her healing process and words were like a balm to my own healing journey. What a beautiful truth to know that I am not alone! Not alone in my struggle, and not alone as I try to dig deeper to find joy within my healing.

I appreciated this book not only because it resonated with my own story, but because it brought both confirmation to things I have already been trying to do, as well as giving me new things I can put into action towards healing even more and learning how to better lean into God through it all.

I highly recommend this book to read and to put on your list of "perfect books to gift to others."

- *Erica A.*

A Time to Dance

Chasing Joy in Difficult Seasons

Shannon Singh

A Time to Dance: Chasing Joy in Difficult Seasons
Copyright © 2022 by Shannon Singh

ISBN: 978-0-578-39300-1 (Paperback Edition)

Visit www.RaisingaBlessing.com
Cover photography by Aaron Singh

First Printing July 2022 / Printed in the United States of America

Dedicated To My Sweet Ryan

When you face difficult seasons in life, experiences or mistakes that leave you broken, angry, or confused, I pray that you always remember this one truth… you are never alone, my love. Your Heavenly Father will scoop you up and hold you as He gently and lovingly pieces you back together.

Life can get really big sometimes, and so incredibly difficult, but we serve a faithful and loving God and He is bigger than anything we face. He goes before us to prepare a way. He works within us to prepare our hearts. And He *will* see you through.

My sweet and beautiful boy, cling to these promises when life leaves you utterly broken-hearted: Jesus sees you. He knows you, individually. He loves you, deeply. And He *will* heal you. And when you find Him there, in the desert or in the wilderness, simply rest in His arms and let Him love on you.

Your daddy and I will always love you wholly, completely, and unconditionally. ♥

We are so very proud of you!

Shine bright, my love!

Chapter 1: The Journey Ahead   3

Chapter 2: Draw Close & Come Just As You Are   11

Chapter 3: Learning to Trust His Voice   20

Chapter 4: Recognizing the Lies Behind Shame   32

Chapter 5: Your Moses Moment   45

Chapter 6: When Feelings Threaten Your Healing   57

Chapter 7: Asking God to Use You   69

Chapter 8: A Pause for Extra   76

Chapter 9: Pray For One Another   78

Chapter 10: The Path to Forgiveness   85

Chapter 11: The God Who Sees You   96

Chapter 12: Step Into Your Authority   119

Chapter 13: Share the Journey   133

Chapter 14: The Painful Why's of Loss   140

Chapter 15: Redefining Perfection   152

Chapter 16: The Brokenness Around You   167

Chapter 17: The Head Bone is Connected to ...   180

Chapter 18: God Doesn't Make Mistakes   199

Chapter 19: Identifying Your Links   205

Chapter 20: Through His Lenses   214

Chapter 21: Your Qualifications for His Kingdom's...   221

Chapter 22: Have Faith, Stay the Course   228

Chapter 23: Sitting in God's Waiting Room   235

Chapter 24: The Joy Journey   247

Chapter 25: There's Power In Your Story   260

Chapter 26: Be the Rare   272

Chapter 27: Into His Healing   280

A Note To My Readers   299

About the Author   301

Chapter 1

The Journey Ahead

O God, be my Savior and rescue me!

*Then he broke through and transformed all my wailing
into a whirling dance of ecstatic praise!*

*He has torn the veil and lifted from me the sad
heaviness of mourning.*

He wrapped me in the glory-garments of gladness.

How could I be silent when it's time to praise you?

*Now my heart sings out, bursting with joy - a bliss inside
that keeps me singing, "I can never thank you enough!"*
(Psalm 30:10-12 TPT)

Take just a moment. Let those verses sit with you.
Really sit with you. Read them again, but slower this
time. Listen for the promise. Give it permission to seep
into your bruised and broken heart today. Then take
that spark of hope and let it encourage and strengthen
you as we begin our journey. The journey through
healing. A journey through the beautiful and the hard.
Speak life into God's promises today.

God, I am giving you my journey today. I am giving you this process knowing that there will be painful and difficult moments but that, if I lean into you, I will leave this season completely transformed. I'm believing in your promises. I am speaking life into them. And as I choose daily to seek your voice, your heart, and your plan, I'm believing that you will...

"(Transform) my wailing,

(Lift) me from the sad heaviness of mourning, (and)

(Wrap) me in ... gladness,

(Until) *my heart sings out, bursting with joy...*

I can never thank you enough!"

As we begin this journey together, I encourage you to believe in one promise, one seed of hope, watering it daily so that it deeply roots in your heart. And that promise is this: We serve an incredible Father. He knows you, individually, and He loves you deeply and unconditionally. He *will* see you through. This season, this pain, even your next step... you will never face any of it alone. He will be your comfort and your guide; your place of rest and your source of strength and fire. He will provide. He will heal. And you *will* dance again. That's His promise to you.

...

I'd like to take just a moment to pause and share with you a sneak peek into what you'll find in the pages ahead. You see, very few (if any) of us will journey through this life without meeting the bathroom floor at some point. Seasons of brokenness affect us all. I say the bathroom floor because that's where I found myself... ugly crying, broken, and lost on the bathroom floor. Sadness, fear, and debilitating anxiety pouring through me. How did I get here? And how will I ever get out?

But in that moment, God reached into my life and held out His hand. "Take just one step with me, my child. Just one. Lean into me. Let me hold you. And when you're ready, we'll take another. Trust me with your heart and we will walk out of this wilderness and step into your healing, hope, peace, and joy... together."

For the better part of the year that followed, I chased His healing, His fire, His joy with great eagerness and intentionality. I held onto His promises like they were *the only thing* that could keep my head above water, the only thing that kept me from drowning. I cried, I screamed, I ached, and I doubted Him. And yet, through it all, He was unwavering in His love and faithfulness and He absolutely changed my life!

He saved me. He poured over me and He held me.

He healed me.

Because of Him, I am a completely different person today than the broken one that He held on that bathroom floor. And my friend, here is His promise: *He will do the same for you.*

But His goodness doesn't end there. In fact, there was another unexpected and seemingly impossible gift of the journey through healing...

A renewed joy like I had never experienced in my life.

It was not a joy that came from a lack of difficulties and hardships. It was a joy deeply rooted in the realization that even on the hardest days, He is for me, He is guiding me, and I can trust in Him and rest in His plan.

The truth is that I did not, and still don't, always know which direction to take, but I have learned to anchor deeply to my relationship with Jesus and allow Him to teach me along the way. And that is why I'm sharing my journey with you... because when we anchor to Him, truly anchor our safety, hope, identity, and peace in Him, joy *will* follow.

You see, when your world is shaken and you find yourself indescribably broken with pieces of your heart shattered and scattered, sometimes it's difficult to believe that you can ever be made whole again. But if I can give you any promise, it's this... He will reach into the rubble and He *will* carry you out.

We serve a God that is always moving, always working behind the scenes. Always present in the details. Always speaking to us and sharing with us pieces of His heart. You are not here (*"here, here"* or *"here on this journey"*) by accident. You found this book because you are meant to be here. We are meant to be here, together. And just as He promised, He is here with us.

He is holding your heart. He knows you by name. He knows exactly what you are facing and what you have already overcome. He is working in the unseen, right now, reweaving your pain and your heartache into something beautiful.

Do not be discouraged. At times, it may feel momentarily uncomfortable, but if we continue to press in, the healing will be absolutely transformational!

Believe this…

The healing that I am speaking of throughout this book …. *it is for you.* Yes, YOU.

Do not let the enemy tell you that this message is meant for everyone else. Do not let him convince you that you are somehow left out, forgotten, alone or unworthy. The truth is… God is right there with you, right now, in your car, in your bedroom, at your work desk, or on your bathroom floor. He is there. And He will make good on His promises.

Life may have bent you. You may never look the same. Forever changed. But He won't let it break you. You will not be lost. *He is there in the bend.* He will hold you as you fall apart. And He will pour His love into you, bringing healing to your heart and slowly piecing you back together.

As you journey through this book, I encourage you to give your pain the space to flow and let the tears land at His feet. He can handle it. *All* of it.

This is not the end of your story and your life will not be defined by this season.

Some days will be hard. Sometimes the only thing we have the strength to do is speak His truths over our journey and allow Him to carry the rest. And that's ok. He is faithful. He will meet you right where you are… in this moment. On this day. And throughout this season.

You see, as I grow daily under the blanket of His grace, I am in constant awe of His goodness and His faithfulness, even in my messiest seasons and even when I doubt Him the most. But there is one more thing that I have also come to realize…

Joy does not come passively.

It's not a season or an emotion. It's a daily choice.

It's a way of walking with Jesus that allows you rest. It's a process of recognizing who you are in Him and dancing in the truth of your beauty. It's the letting go. It's the learning to lean in. It's facing the hard things and putting them where they belong. It's the re-defining of who you are. It's opening your heart and letting Jesus show you His plan. It's taking back power from the enemy and knowing your strength and authority in Jesus.

It's the little actions we take every day to change how we process and react to the world around us.

It's peace, strength, grace, and love! And that is what Jesus wants for you ... and with you!

He wants to deepen His relationship with you. He wants you to find rest in His promises and to dance in celebration of His goodness. He has gone before you to prepare the way and He has a plan. All that He is asking of you is to take that first step in faith. He will light the path and He will prepare you for the journey.

Fall into Him today and know that *you will be healed.* There is hope for a better tomorrow. Cling to Him and speak life into your healing with the words of His promises. Take my hand and we will step into His healing together. I am praying for you today. From my heart to yours, blessings on the journey ahead.

From my heart
To yours...

Blessings on
the journey ahead.

– Shannon

Chapter 2

Draw Close &
Come Just As You Are

I'm so glad that you are here! Truly! And because I deeply respect and honor your journey, I wanted to get one little important confession out of the way right up front... one little (not-so-little) clarification and detail for the road ahead. So here it is...

This "Chasing Joy" journey is not about what *knowledge* I can offer you. Far from it. No, the truth is I'm in the trenches with you, still learning and growing every day. And although I have faced seasons that left me defeated, deeply injured, and scarred, I have not walked in your shoes. I cannot fathom or understand the pain that you have faced. No, this journey is not about what *I* can offer you. But this journey does start with another woman... The bleeding woman in the crowd.

You see, in the Gospel of Mark, we find Jesus traveling from town to town, ministering and performing miracles. Large crowds were gathering to see and hear whatever they could. Now, take a moment and imagine how difficult it must have been to even get a glimpse of Jesus, even more difficult if you were at the back of the crowd. But here was this woman. She had suffered for years from a bleeding disease and although she had seen many doctors, her condition worsened. I imagine she was weak, tired, and felt hopeless. But when she heard about Jesus, she took every last bit of faith and strength that she had left and pushed with all her might through the large, loud, seemingly impassible crowd just to draw close to Him and touch the hem of His garment. And she was healed.

Two powerful words: *Draw Close.* That is what He is calling us to do on this journey. He wants to heal us. He wants to use our hard for good. He wants to love us deeply and remind us who we are in Him. He wants to give us joy, purpose, a renewed spark, and a place where we belong and shine! He wants us to dance again!

And much like this woman, there may be times in this process when we feel hopeless, get shoved to the ground, feel overwhelmed by the impossible (or seemingly impassible), or just simply grow weary from the journey, but He is calling us to… *draw close…* and believe.

Daughter, because you dared to believe, your faith has healed you. Go with peace in your heart, and be free from your suffering! (Mark 5:34 TPT)

Therefore, I cannot and could not have started this process without first starting with Jesus. He is the One True Healer.

But as you'll soon see, there is more to learn from the bleeding woman in the crowd...so much more!

I'll probably never forget the day that I was knee-deep into a conversation about unforgiveness with my counselor. She knew that the unforgiveness was causing my heart to harbor anger. I knew that holding onto anger wouldn't bring me any closer to finding joy. And yet, we found ourselves at this crossroad with no clear direction on where to go. So, she made a suggestion:

"Why don't you try acting out a conversation with this person, Shannon? Place a pillow in a chair and tell it (them) what you really want to say, deep inside."

"I can't do that."

"Why?"

"Because God wouldn't like me to say all of those things. He would be disappointed in me. In my heart."

She paused for a moment and looked right at me, "Shannon, God already knows what is in your heart."

Whoa.

A wave of total shame poured over me. You see, I thought that by not speaking it, I had somehow hidden this "stuff" away from God so that He would be proud of how I was holding it all together to serve Him. But that illusion was quickly fading as the truth in her words began to sink in... He could see it all along. And suddenly, I felt very ashamed.

Funny how that's always my knee-jerk reaction: shame. In fact, we will chat quite a bit more about shame in chapter four, but back to my conversation with my counselor that day...

It took me a while to move beyond the shame and truly process what she had said. *God could see the messy unforgiveness and anger in my heart all along, and yet, He still chose to pour His love over me.*

He still sought my heart and held me close. He met me there, right where I was, and He loved me just the same. So really, by trying to hide this unforgiveness, I wasn't preventing Him from knowing it was there. I was only preventing Him from moving through it with His healing touch.

And suddenly, I'm looped back to the bleeding woman. (*I told you there was more!*)

If you're new to the story, don't worry... so was I. But as God took me on this journey over the last year, He spoke to me about the bleeding woman often. Let's dive in a little deeper and you'll understand why...

Now, in the crowd that day was a woman who had suffered horribly from continual bleeding for twelve years. She had endured a great deal under the care of various doctors, yet in spite of spending all she had on their treatments, she was getting worse instead of better. (Mark 5:25-26 TPT)

Because these two verses don't necessarily give you the full picture, I'd like to attempt to describe this woman in more detail. A bleeding disorder like hers would have likely meant total ostracization from family and community. You see, due to her disease, she was said to be unclean. And worse, she could make others unclean with her touch or presence. So, for twelve years this hurting woman had likely not felt the warmth of a hug.

As I process that, I simply cannot imagine how broken my heart would feel. She had suffered a great deal physically and could not be comforted in the arms of another as she cried. She must have been so desperate for His healing touch when she heard that Jesus was walking by!

Then I picture what she must have looked like. Ostracization surely meant that all other hygiene practices were likely extremely limited. I'm sure her clothes were tattered and torn. I imagine that her body was covered in dirt, or worse. Years of bleeding and no proper access to the cleansing practices of her times likely caused an odor that she was completely helpless to remedy. I wonder if her hair was matted. I wonder if her face showed signs of a woman who had been weathered and broken. It truly squeezes my heart to imagine her this way, but this was likely her reality, however unimaginable it may feel.

Then I wonder ...

What if she had looked down at herself and thought... I cannot come to Jesus like this!

What if she had left to try and quickly wash herself first?

Would she have missed Him walking by?

Would she have been so busy trying to make herself good enough for Him that she missed her healing entirely?

And more importantly, did He expect that of her?

I'm going to sit with that last question for just a moment because I find myself relating to it more and more.

I think we know the answer...

Then Jesus said to her, "Daughter, because you dared to believe, your faith has healed you. Go with peace in your heart, and be free from your suffering!" (Mark 5:34 TPT)

And in that one verse, I realize...

He didn't feel repulsed.

He didn't turn away.

He didn't condemn her for approaching Him so "unclean."

And He certainly didn't tell her to come back when she's a better version of herself.

And He won't for me. And He won't for you.

He isn't asking us to bring the best version of ourselves to His table. He isn't asking us to get all of our ducks in a row before we touch the fringe of His garment. He doesn't need us to clear all the other clutter and come to Him with our hearts pure and ready. We are trying so hard to clean up this mess, all this dirt and all this debris, to prepare ourselves for Him and to make ourselves "good enough." But my friends...

He is walking by... right now!

Look up and just run to Him.

For just a moment, forget about the odor that your unclean makes and just let Him hold you and heal you. He isn't asking us for anything else. The first thing that God spoke to me about the bleeding woman in the crowd was that above all else, she prioritized these two words... *draw close.* Not cleansing. Not making herself worthy. Not being good enough. Not trying to be perfect. Simply this... Draw close and come just as you are. *Bring the authentic you.*

Throughout this journey, He will be pouring over us with His unconditional love, covering us in His grace and reminding us that we are His cherished possession, but there may still be things in our heart that we hesitate to give Him because we feel ashamed. There may be pieces of us that we resist letting Him touch because we feel the need to clean them up first. There may still be a part of us that holds back because we just don't have it all together... all ready yet... and we think surely He would look at us with total discontent (or worse) and tell us to come back when we are more prepared.

Trust me, I understand. It took me a long time to let Him into my unforgiveness and my anger. To let Him work through them and within me. To truly bring my authentic self and allow Him to begin the deep healing process.

I held back so much for so long because I thought I *needed* to keep it under wraps. I thought that by not naming it, not admitting it, even to myself, I would make Him proud. I would be the good and kind-hearted follower that He wanted. But as I reflect back on that difficult time in my process, I slowly begin to realize that the only thing it truly served to accomplish was the blocking of His healing power moving through it. Moving through me. And He definitely wasn't asking for that.

But guess what... He is still working in it today, patiently and lovingly walking me through the process. It's a journey, and I now know that He will love me no less for it and no more for the healing of it. I will always be wholly, immensely, and unconditionally loved just as much by my Heavenly Father that proudly calls me His.

So, I encourage you today to simply and beautifully take this first step with me and draw close. Fall into Him. Bring the authentic you. He can handle it and He will never walk away.

Let Him love you just as you are, your beauty *and* the things that you work so hard to hide. Because when you let Him have it all, you begin to truly realize and understand that He loves you the same today. Tomorrow. And always. And that truth, rooted deeply into your heart, will produce the faith and courage to push through the crowd, like the bleeding woman, and draw ever closer to Him, the One True Healer.

Chapter 3

Learning to Trust
His Voice

Throughout the course of this journey, you'll hear me talk a lot about the disciple and fisherman, Peter. You see, I think there's a very powerful question hidden in his story that gives me pause to really think about who God is and what He promises. And as I explore the answer to that question more deeply, it truly helps me redefine my focus, particularly in difficult seasons. Allow me to explain...

On a recent trip to the beach, my father and I sat outside at the grill one afternoon discussing the story of Peter walking on water. It may sound like an odd combination, but I kid you not, as the delicious smell of wild grouse, bell peppers, and onions filled the air, we sat there pondering and discussing a very deep question. Hours later, the question still lingered in my mind as I dipped my toes in the sand and watched the waves of an incoming storm beat against the shore. I couldn't help but realize the importance of its answer and its relevance to the journey that we are on today. And that deep and revealing question was this:

What would make you step out of that boat?

Raging seas. Huge waves. A very powerful and threatening storm. And there was Jesus. *"Trust me. Believe that I love you. Let go. Fall into Me."*

And as I stood there, watching and listening to the waves of this incoming storm slam against the sand, I wondered… *"What would it take for me to step out of that boat?"*

What about you?

What would it take to fully let go and fall into His arms? What storm are you facing right now that has left you bruised and in pain? What fear is holding your heart hostage?

Jesus, I'm scared. Jesus, I'm trembling inside. I feel lost and alone; ashamed and buried. Jesus, I'm being crushed under all this weight. I want to give it all to you, I really do… but I just don't know how.

Can I make a suggestion? We are not expected to blindly trust or release control into the hands of a God that we don't know.

We have a handwritten letter with our name on it; a personal and sincere invitation from the One who loves us most. An invitation to deepen our *relationship* with Him. It's an opportunity to let Him love you, heal you, and show you (*or remind you*) who you are and Whose you are.

And friends, here's the real truth… it's a journey that will allow the trust, and the stepping out, to become a natural extension of our relationship with Him as we grow to understand and deeply know Who it is that we are stepping out of the boat towards and just how much He loves us.

If needed, take a quick pause and read that sentence again, as many times as it takes to let it deeply root in your heart. Feel the weight lift and let the guilt and pressure fall. It's not about knowing *who* He is and willing the faith to follow, but rather taking steps towards truly *knowing* Him. It's not about what *we* can do to overcome fear. It's about what He can do within us when we choose to grow in our love and connection with Him first and allow the rest to develop naturally.

Here's the bottom line… You don't have to carry the heavy and defeating motto of willing yourself into submission. You don't have to believe the lie that you need to work harder to be a better believer. *It doesn't work.* You don't need to fake it until you make it, faith it into fruition, or pretend that you're not scared. He is not asking you for any of that.

The key words here are: *Know Him*. He is asking us to lean deeply into our *relationship* with Him so we may truly *feel* His heart, *personally experience* His presence and intimately *know Him*.

He is very alive and His presence is a tangible part of my day when it fills my space. And when we focus on our relationship with Him, instead of the storm, we are reminded that He is a loving Father, a provider (even when the way seems impassible to our eyes), a protector, and a tender voice that encourages our hearts and blankets our pain and fear with His touch.

It doesn't mean the storm always calms. It means as you allow Him to show you who He is and how much He loves you, over and over, you'll find that placing your heart in His hands will begin to occur naturally. It's not a forced action or a submission of willpower, but a welcomed fruit of your *personal experience* of God's goodness. And then, you will begin to step out of the boat during even the most difficult storms because you remember…

I know that man Jesus. I love Him and He loves me. And I trust Him.

He is speaking to our hearts right now… *"Fall into me. Let Me hold you. Don't fear where I'm taking you. I have gone before you and I'm already there. I have prepared a way and I'm preparing you."*

And all He is asking of us is to press into growing closer to Him and allow Him to work through the rest.

Knowing His Voice

But before we go any further, I want to take a pause here for a moment because I hear your question and your heart, and I've been there too.

I want to do this. I want to fully fall in. But, how does this life-changing process of truly knowing Him begin? Knowing His heart, personally experiencing His love, and having that deeply intimate relationship with Him? Where do I even start?

For just a moment, I'd like to loop us back to the story of Peter, particularly Peter's response when the disciples saw Jesus walking on the water towards their boat:

Then Peter called to Him, "Lord, if it's really you, tell me to come to you, walking on the water." (Matthew 14:28 NLT)

"Lord, if it's really you... tell me..."

Because that's a key piece of the puzzle too, isn't it? Hearing His voice. Knowing His voice. Becoming familiar with His voice. So that we can trust in His voice.

And yet, this piece of the puzzle is sometimes the most difficult part to truly lean into and fully trust. If we had Jesus standing in front of us telling us to step out, some of us might leap over the boat railing faster than we've ever leapt before. But there's something about trusting a voice from a source that we cannot see that makes our heart take pause and doubt.

Is that really Him? Or is it me?

How do I know?

I'm scared to trust and lean in because what if I'm wrong and it's not Him?

I don't want to look stupid.

I don't want to fail.

I don't want to mess this up.

Ugh. This is so hard.

And we stay in that place of uncertainty, frozen in fear-induced immobility, as our God-given opportunities (or calling) wait. I have been there, too. Many times. And hear my heart on this: There is no shame in that place, but there *is* opportunity.

You see, when God has asked me to step out, I have often found myself asking, *"Is this you? I don't know. This seems so... uncomfortable. And I'm sure if this really was you, you would choose someone better. Someone more equipped. Someone more qualified. This must be me just thinking it's you. Yeah... I'm sure it's just me... and not you, God."*

Ok. Good chat.

Right?

And sometimes this topic makes us squirm in discomfort, feeling like we are somehow sinning by doubting God's voice and we are a disappointment to Him. But that's simply not true.

Learning His voice is a natural part of the growing process in our relationship with Him. I've sat in that doubt and sometimes still do. But guess what? He meets me there, every time, lovingly and patiently teaching me and guiding me through it. He allows me the space to grow and learn about who He is and how much He loves me. And in that growth, I learn to trust Him and His voice more and more.

Again, the *relationship* becomes the key. The trusting Him, and His voice, become the natural and easy byproduct of growing to know His heart. It all starts with *knowing* Him.

So, what do we do? When He speaks to us, how do we begin to truly recognize and trust His voice? How do we become so familiar with His voice that we do not need to *see* Him in order to run towards Him with the same zeal?

The answer is both beautiful and simple... we allow Him to teach us!

God loves us and He delights in His relationship with us. He will guide us as we lean in and seek Him. And as we become more familiar with His voice, we will become more confident in our trust of it.

So, if you're finding that this piece of the puzzle is something that you are struggling with today, here are some easy steps and words of encouragement that you can press into:

1. First and foremost, I encourage you to NOT create filters or expectations based on other's experiences. One of the beautiful things about our Heavenly Father is that He knows us, intimately and individually. And He speaks to us in our own ways. One of the biggest barriers that we can create between His voice and our trust is when we expect to see or hear Him in the same way that another does. When we begin to trust that He speaks to us in our own individual way, it allows us to experience Him more freely and frequently within us and around us.

2. Pray and ask for confirmation. There have been many times when I felt hesitant or confused. *Am I really hearing you, God?* It is not a question that carries any guilt or shame. When this feeling causes me to take pause or to doubt, I simply stop and pray over His message. He will always be faithful to show you that it is His voice, often through another person, a song, an encounter, a moment, or a divine experience. Trust Him to reassure your heart without fearing Him finding fault in your question or doubt.

3. Speak to Him regularly. I speak with God like I'm calling up my mom on the phone. I talk to Him about my day. About my fears. About my dreams. I talk to Him in the car. In the shower. While I'm working in the yard. The more we spend time with Him, the more natural the relationship feels. He's not a God that sits above, all powerful, waiting for moments

when we drop the ball, fail, or start to sink. He's a Father who delights in the sharing of our every day, our ordinary, and having a relationship with us. Speak to Him on your drive to pick up the kids from school or on your lunch break at work. Call on Him, whisper a prayer, and have a quick chat. He loves it! He loves you!

4. Write it down! Oh, how I love this! When you feel Him speaking to you, be intentional about writing it down. You never know when God will use it later to provide confirmation of His word.

About a year ago, God gave me a message. The message related directly to His calling on my heart and a future role in ministry. I pondered heavily on His words, unable to fully invest in the belief that I had heard Him right. To be honest, I completely doubted the message and almost dismissed the idea altogether. A few days later, I came across something that I had written in my Bible thirteen years before. Thirteen years prior, but with the EXACT same message from God. A divine peek into my future, a promise, a calling, and a confirmation all in one. Whoa!

There is tremendous power in writing down His words to you! Write them down and watch them come to fruition. He is a faithful and good Father! Want to grow in confidence that you are hearing Him? Begin to write it down and pray over it!

5. When you feel His nudges, take the time to dig deeper. Whether He lays a Bible verse on your heart, a song on your mind, or a person in your thoughts, take the time to press in. When I started this book, I had some fears about knowing what to write. I was driving one day, heavy with nerves about it all, and I felt Him press the verse James 1:5 on my heart. I decided to pull over and look it up.

"If you need wisdom, ask our generous God, and he will give it to you. He will not rebuke you for asking." NLT

Wow! How relevant. And how moving. Suddenly, I realized that He was reminding me to rest in His promise that He would be with me throughout the process. And that's just one example. Want to grow in confidence that you are feeling His nudges? Dig deeper when He presses.

6. Don't allow the enemy to place thoughts into your mind that block God's messages from reaching your heart. Thoughts like, *"you aren't good enough or worthy enough. He wouldn't be speaking to you or pouring into you. You simply don't deserve it."* Maybe this isn't a barrier for everyone, but for some of us, we struggle to believe that we deserve to have God's blessings and favor in our lives; that we are somehow not worthy of His presence and His love. But this is simply not true. God loves you more than you can imagine. Don't talk yourself out of believing you hear His voice because you feel

undeserving or because the enemy is whispering lies over your identity and your place in the Kingdom. You are God's cherished possession, His beautiful child. Wanted. Sought After. Loved. And Belonging.

7. Do not convince yourself that you must be hearing Him wrong if He's calling you to do something big. You are never too small or too unqualified for whatever God has in store! He will equip you. He will provide you with everything you need. He has already placed treasures inside of you that have yet to be discovered. If you feel small, get ready... He's about to show you how amazing you really are! How amazing He really is! Never feel too small to accomplish whatever He is placing on your heart!

My prayer is that this journey will allow you to see and feel His presence more and more. I hope that you hear Him speaking into your heart daily, calling you into His plans for your life. I encourage you to use a journal to document His love notes, His messages, and His presence. He's there, always.

He enters our space and speaks to our hearts because He wants to deepen our relationship with Him. We are His family. He desires to pour out His love over us; to overflow our cup. He doesn't just want our worship and praise. He wants us to *know* Him and love Him on a much deeper level.

And friends, if we pause and listen, in the hard, in the easy, in the everyday, and even in the mundane, we will hear Him.

Lean in and allow His voice to become a steady and calming reassurance of His presence, His love, and His faithfulness. Fall in love with Him, daily, and everything else will grow naturally.

Chapter 4

Recognizing The Lies Behind Shame

Late summer two years ago, I found myself driving one of our local mountain passes right at sunset. The pink alpenglow had just begun to fill the evening sky and the clouds were breathtaking. I decided to pull over into one of the popular scenic overlook spots and just pause for a moment in the chaos of life to take it all in. As I stood there, completely in awe of the view in front of me, I heard God enter my thoughts and tenderly whisper, *"give it to me."*

His voice caught me by complete surprise. In a season that had been filled with so many *what if's,* I was actually taking in a moment and trying to force myself to sit in the space of *what is. So,* when He stepped into that moment, that place of breathtaking beauty in the middle of utter chaos, I wasn't really sure where His conversation was headed and, to be honest, I wasn't sure I was ready for the answer. In what probably sounded like a sigh of utter defeat, sadness, and exhaustion, I simply responded back, "give you what?"

"Your shame."

My reaction was quick and unwavering, requiring little to no thought...

"I can't, God. I deserve it. If people knew what I was really like, they would say the same."

My heart sank as all of the painful reminders and memories quickly passed through my head. Shame had come to define me. There wasn't a corner of my life untouched by its mark. It was heavy. So heavy. And the truth was, it had defeated me long ago.

But again, I felt Him gently press...

"Give it to me."

...

Shame. How many of us carry it? And though some of us carry it better than others, the weight of it is still there, threatening to drag us under at any moment. It's defining. It's limiting. It's fear-inducing. And... it's in the way.

You see, we cannot find true joy unless we give the enemy back everything that belongs to him and one of the first things we need to give back is shame.

Shame is one of the enemy's most powerful and effective tools. Why? Because it leads us to inaction due to our feelings of unworthiness.

Do not believe for one moment that the enemy thinks you insignificant. Far from it. You see, when God created you, He gave you an incredibly special and unique calling, along with the power and authority to walk in it. You were chosen. You are one-of-a-kind. You are far from unimportant. And you are definitely not cookie cutter.

You are called by name and your role in His kingdom is irreplaceable. Your heart is His desire and He has a plan designed just for you. You have a divine and powerful purpose... *And the enemy knows it.*

So, what does the enemy do to destroy you? He lies. He tells you that you are not worthy. You're not good enough. You've fallen short. You have run too far. Your grace period has ended. You are a disappointment. Jesus gave up on you. God literally threw His hands in the air and He walked away.

And he, the enemy, is a liar.

Harsh language? Perhaps. But let me tell you first-hand how easy it is to accept that you deserve to walk in that shame. So, while I may sound harsh, it's important to understand... The enemy *is* a liar. And he seeks, right now, to absolutely destroy your heart.

And while we're on this topic, let me tell you something else the enemy knows. Something that is so powerful and completely life-changing that he will undoubtedly do anything to keep you from believing it...

He, the enemy, has absolutely no power or authority over you except what he can convince you to accept.

So, what does he do? He manipulates. He uses our most vulnerable, tender, and painful areas and seasons to twist us into knots of insecurity, fear, anxiety, and shame.

Shame. There's that word again. The truth is, the enemy will use every mistake, every painful word spoken over us, every misstep, and every situation or season that has left us feeling broken or flawed to keep us in a tormenting cycle of shame.

But why? Why is the enemy so focused on little, insignificant me?

Because if he can succeed in convincing us that we are (in fact) small, insignificant, unworthy, irrelevant, or broken, then he will absolutely use those labels to effectively build a solid case against us, and worse, against God. *He will attempt to wrap those words, those labels, so tightly around our identity that they become chains that hold us back from ever accepting and walking in our God-given identity, beauty, purpose, worth, and calling!*

But hear this again… You have *absolute* authority over the enemy. Not just a little. Not just enough. *Absolute authority.* And taking back that authority, giving him back what belongs to him, starts with recognizing his lies:

- The enemy will always make you feel insignificant and small. God will *never* label you as unworthy or irrelevant. We are chosen, His family, His children, and that unwavering love, that unconditional belonging, *will never change.*

- The enemy will always remind you of your mistakes, imperfections, and insecurities to make you feel unworthy, weighed down, and held back. The truth is, you are covered in grace, set free by the blood of Jesus, and there isn't a moment that He doesn't call you beautiful, whole, forgiven and redeemed. *Truth: There is no list of your exceptions to His grace… but the one that the enemy keeps.*

- The enemy will always make you feel hopeless and alone. There is nothing further from the truth… ever! God's truth says you are never alone. He will never leave you, fail you, or abandon you. Just look at Isaiah 46:4, Isaiah 43:2, and Deuteronomy 31:6. In Him, you can safely and confidently place all your hope because He is with you, always.

- The enemy will try to use past seasons of hurt to keep you in a cycle of defeat and exhaustion. Your

Heavenly Father can, and will, help you defeat those destructive lies of bondage and entrapment with His life-giving truths. What the enemy attempts to defeat and destroy, God came to heal, redeem, and breathe life back into: you. And He *will* see you through.

- The enemy will always use any tool he can to convince us that we have failed God, or worse, that God has failed us. Don't let the enemy *ever* tell you who God is or who you are in Him. Our identity rests in God, and God alone. If you ever question who He is or who you are in Him, all you need is ask. Your Heavenly Father will undoubtedly meet your question with His unfailing love and you will understand that your place in His heart and His kingdom is irreplaceable.

I imagine that as some of you are reading through these truths today, you are beginning to feel that nudge from the Holy Spirit saying the enemy has been lying to you, manipulating you, or cycling you through seasons of pain and shame. If that's the case, I encourage you, right now, to take that first step in authority over him. Whisper a prayer to your Heavenly Father. Curl up at His feet and let Him hold you. Place these lies, these identity-crushing cycles, in His hands. And as you seek shelter under His wings, you will find that His voice will begin to break through the enemy's cruel words and speak truth into your broken heart...

You are not only worthy, you were chosen!

You were not only chosen, you are deeply cherished!

We belong. You, my friend... you belong. I belong. We are a crucial part of His family.

We are forgiven, loved, and made flawless. Flawless!

He has a future for you filled with hope, peace, and joy!

You are His heart. *His whole heart.*

There is always a place for you at His table. Just for you. Because you belong. Always.

Believe this: You were worth His greatest sacrifice, His total and complete incredible act of love... *and you still are today.*

The List

But what if you are reading those words... *chosen, forgiven, cherished*, and you still feel something else entirely? What if you feel unworthy, confused, unsteady, or unsure? What if you feel torn and you find yourself going back and forth between His truths and the enemy's lies and you aren't sure which one to believe?

I have been there too and that's when God guided me to make a list. *The* list. And it quickly became a significant and frequently-revisited part of my healing.

What list am I talking about? A list of all of the words that are tattooed on my heart and have become deeply woven into the core of my identity.

The *circumstances* that I felt had defined me.

The *opinions of others* that were poured like concrete into my heart, weighing down my spirit and diminishing my joy because I still carried them.

The *mistakes* that I had made.

The *seasons* that had changed me.

The *hurt and pain* that had labeled me and kept me stuck in a cycle of doubt, fear, and insecurity.

The *brand* with which the enemy had kept me enslaved. The one- or two-word reminders that sucked me back under that dark cloud, sometimes for days.

The good and the beautiful. The pain and the joy. The truths and the lies. He told me to write them all.

I knew it would be hard, but I also knew I was ready. I knew that He had not only brought me to this place, but He had prepared my heart for the journey ahead.

In truth, there were times that I used a pencil because the heaviness of ink felt like more than I could handle, but I didn't leave anything unsaid.

You see, I knew that I would be taking my list to Jesus. I knew that I would be laying it at His feet and listening for His heart. So, I let the walls down, allowed the vulnerability to flow, and I wrote it all.

I prayed over all of them. I wept over some of them. And in all honesty, I completely broke over a few of them. Crashed and crumbled. Curled up in the fetal position, desperately wanting to run or hide. But here's the beautiful truth... Like the gentle and loving Father that He is, He would always meet me there, reminding me why He was calling me to face this difficult and painful part of the process and encouraging me to draw strength from His presence and His promises; pressing me to keep leaning in. And as I began to ask Him to move through my list, move through me, and reveal His truths and His heart, I discovered that the process of the list became truly life-changing.

If you're reading this chapter and planning to make your own list, let me encourage your heart...

It's the painful ones that come to mind first and oh, how heavy they feel to actually write down. The way your heart squeezes and your stomach drops. The way the weight of the memory threatens to pull you under and drown you. And in that moment, you'll find yourself wanting to turn back, I understand. I am truly so sorry for your pain. But if you can hit pause for just a moment, I promise you this... He is with you, guiding you through this hard, and you will walk away completely transformed. Catch your breath, take heart, and press on.

Push through the discomfort and walk with me. We are not bound by these words, these mistakes, these seasons, anymore. *This is our goodbye letter.* We are laying our lists at the feet of Jesus and praying over them. It's time to give the enemy back all that is his and take back our authority and *our true identity* in Jesus.

> *God, I know (insert your word) is not how you see me. I know that it is a lie that the enemy has whispered into my thoughts so many times that I have allowed it to become a destructive and defeating label that I now use for myself. Help me to erase this word from my identity and replace it with a name that you call me. Show me who I am in your eyes. And as I walk through my day, please reveal your truths to me so that I may understand and find rest in them.*

You see, as you journey through your list, God will begin to plant seeds in your heart. New words, His words. Be intentional about watering them in your spirit. Declare His truths to be your truths. Make them daily affirmations. Post yourself a sticky note on your mirror, write them down in your journal, or set a reminder on your phone.

There's something so powerful about putting ink to paper. Sometimes these small physical actions can bring huge spiritual breakthroughs. Write it down... You are chosen. You are wanted. And you are deeply, unconditionally, and immeasurably loved.

Make that your proclamation today! Because we are ONLY defined by Him. Our identity begins and ends with our Heavenly Father, today and every day.

Healed, Forgiven, Redeemed, *Erased*

Are you feeling hopeful? I pray that you do. I pray that you feel His promise pressing on your heart and I hope it's encouraging you in your own journey. But before we move forward, I wanted to take a moment and share a gentle reminder, another very important nugget of truth that I learned along the way.

The truth is, as you walk through this process and you begin to feel healing and hope pour into the cracks and crevices in your heart and your identity, you may (at times) also begin to feel an internal battle rising.

Be on alert for these whispers, these challenges to your growth, these internal collisions between the old and the new. Revisit your list and take a moment to truly evaluate the root cause of the conflict. Ask yourself…

Where is this rooted?

Who is reminding me?

Is it God's truth?

And do I want to water it?

Believe me when I say that God knows your heart. He has seen every step of your journey. He has watched your struggle. He has seen the good and the ugly. And He *is* a proud father, still today, when He says, "*you are mine.*" Those are the truths that we need to grab and hold onto. Those are the truths with which we are invited to safely anchor our identity.

Therefore, remember this when you face the internal struggle between the evicted and the newly planted; when you reexamine your list and discover old words being rewritten on your heart and rewoven into your identity; when you feel the familiar tug that says you are not worthy or you don't belong...

God will never ask you to rewrite something that He has already erased. It's gone. It's buried. It's forgiven, redeemed, and made flawless.

The enemy, on the other hand, is never above lying and dragging you back into that old, painful, and familiar cycle of shame by whatever means possible.

Recognize it for what it is and then pour yourself back into what God is saying about you. Take the shame that the enemy is using to hold you back and give it to Jesus. You may have to do this over and over, but don't stop.

Jesus came to heal you and lift you out of the lie that you are not enough. He chose you. He stood in the gap for you. And you are worthy. Today. Yesterday. On your worst day. And tomorrow, still.

Even the ugliest words, the ugliest mistakes, or the ugliest scars on your list... placed in His hands, they can be reweaved into something healing and so powerful. The work that He is doing in your heart right now will become your testimony. Hold onto hope. He is with you, always.

Leave Room for Grace

I wanted to take a moment and share one last note before we leave this chapter; one last beautiful and important message of encouragement for your heart. I know that we've walked through a lot so far. I recognize that creating the list that we discussed in this chapter may be incredibly hard and challenging for you. So, friends...

Remember to leave room for grace... for yourself.

The truth is, you may find yourself looping back, rewriting old words that He has erased, laying it down at His feet only to pick it back up again. And that's okay.

If you stumble, if you trip over an old word and find yourself face down in the dirt, take a moment to pause and allow yourself space to grieve and process. Then, when you're ready, remind yourself why you're here, *remind yourself Who is with you,* dust off, and begin the work again.

Chapter 5

Your Moses Moment

For the authority of her faith rested in the One who made the promise, and she tapped into his faithfulness.

(Hebrews 11:11 TPT)

One of the most challenging barriers to joy is the often-overwhelming thought of *"how?"* I have frequently faced this doubt in my own journey and today I am sharing with you a very real and raw look into what Jesus has been teaching me about *"faith like Moses."* To be honest, just a short while ago, I would have thought sharing such an intimate part of my journey would make me feel too vulnerable. But now, I'm dusting off my dancing shoes and waiting for the fulfillment of His promises… God is good, my friends!

On a random drive in April last year, my husband pointed out an old bridge on the side of the road. He knows I can't resist old bridges, barns, mountains, and well, anything with that *farm* or *farmhouse in the mountains* feel. I looked over with eager anticipation of what he was pointing out. What I never expected was to have God step into that moment and give me a vision. And not just any vision… a promise. A very special promise.

You see, instead of simply seeing an old bridge beautifully placed in a grassy country field, what I saw in that moment was…

Me…

On that very old bridge…

Spinning.

Like a carefree child, I was just spinning. My hair was blowing. My heart was lifted. One glance and you could see the genuine, authentic, and deeply rooted joy that spread across my face and overflowed. Happiness. Peace. Hope. Fullness.

And then I saw my skirt. It was a long, white flowing skirt with brightly colored flowers spread all over it. The flowers danced as I spun and the entire vision was just beautiful and breathtaking.

Then I heard God whisper…

"This is my promise to you."

When the vision ended, I couldn't speak. I couldn't move. This was my first experience with a God-given vision and I was quite overwhelmed with emotion.

It took me several days to confide in my husband about what had happened on that drive. Why? Because once my feet hit the ground again, once my brain began to truly process His message that day, I found myself facing bucket-loads of doubt. In fact, that's probably an understatement. Doubt or the other "D" word... disbelief? I quite literally asked God, "*how?!*"

You see, I could not envision a path that led me from this dark place that I felt all the way down to my bones to where He was showing me, promising me, that He was taking me. It just didn't make sense when I tried to process it through my own life-experience filter, and I honestly wasn't sure how I felt about that.

Each time I revisited the vision in my mind, I would argue with God. *"But Jesus, I'm too broken. The scars run too deep. I've been hurt too much to ever find my way back. I'm too damaged and I'll never find that kind of joy again. There is no realistic road that leads to that promise. I can understand and accept*  *a path to happiness again, sure. But joy? Childlike joy? Heart-lifting, life-changing, skirt-spinning joy?"* No, I decided that I could not bring myself to believe in that. It simply felt like too much to ask.

One of the things I love about having a relationship with my Heavenly Father is that I've come to realize that He never leaves us on the journey alone, even in moments like those when I doubt Him the most. Instead, when my grief and disbelief felt overwhelming on that day, He stepped into my thoughts once more and taught me another lesson about His ever-present faithfulness.

Remember the story of Moses and the Red Sea? The Israelites were escaping slavery. The enemy, the king's army, was chasing them and they were afraid. As we know from the story, they had every right to be frightened because, by all accounts, they were completely trapped. They faced the Red Sea and realized that there was no way out. There was quite literally *no path* that led them from where they were standing in that moment to the other side. But here's the game-changing detail... there *was* a promise. And God, in all His faithfulness, made good on His promise and created a perfect path where just moments before, there was nothing. They stepped out in faith and they found themselves on completely different ground, their enemies crushed behind them.

Read that last line again... *They stepped out in faith and they found themselves on completely different ground.*

God made a way.

See where I'm going with this? When God gave me a vision last year and told me where He was taking me, I quite literally cried out "*how?*" I couldn't see a path from the dark place where I was standing to the joy that He was promising.

In fact, here's an excerpt from my own personal journal after God gave me that vision:

I'm broken. Like really, really broken. Where there once stood a confident, fun, and playful woman, there now stands a shell. I have become an empty cavern, my laughter like a distant memory of someone else entirely. My light spirit and glow have been replaced by a dark, heavy cloud that seems to push me deeper into depression and non-existence. Though I fight at times to be the diamond that I once was, I often succumb to the pain and my light disappears again.
Will I ever find my way back?

In my darkest days, I literally feel like someone has used a spoon and carved out everything inside me, at least all the beautiful parts. I can't focus. I can't breathe. I can't eat. I can't stop crying and I can't cry anymore, all at the same time. I have panic attacks, fear, anger, insecurity, and anxiety beyond comprehension. My soul feels crushed and I feel… broken.

And then, there is Jesus. In the middle of what feels like never-ending waves in a huge storm,

one that I feel too weak to fight, and He is giving me a promise. A light. And suddenly it has become my mission to find out how to get from this deep, dark hole to that place that I saw in the vision. It has become my mission to walk in His purpose and find my way back. He is going to make something good from this.
And I am going to dance!

Maybe you are feeling that way right now. Or maybe you feel like you are standing in the wilderness, alone and unnoticed. Maybe you too struggle with feelings of hopelessness and fear? Maybe you look at this mess all around you and think, I'll never be the same. I'll never heal. I'll never recover.

Sometimes I thought the wilderness would swallow me up whole and I would cease to exist, at least emotionally and spiritually. But, hear His promise...

We serve a Heavenly Father that will find us, even in the wilderness, make that *especially* in the wilderness, and He will pour His heart over us. He will remind us who we are and Whose we are. And if we lean into His goodness and His promises, we will leave this wilderness completely transformed!

I will be transformed.

You *will* be transformed.

He *will* make a way.

You see, when difficult seasons leave us beaten and bruised, it's so easy to feel unnoticed, unheard, and even misunderstood. But you are *never* unseen or unheard by the One that loves you the most. He is there. In the little. In the big. In the seen. And in the unseen. And He loves you.

Whatever you are facing today that is keeping you from believing that such joy is attainable for you, give it to God. Don't listen to the enemy's lies and taunts that you will be forever trapped in this season. *God can make a path and you can be standing on completely different ground tomorrow!*

Ask God to show you His promises for your life and your future and then believe it. Receive it. Rest in it. Find hope in it. And speak life into it. Then just watch what God can do with your faith!

…

Now, are you ready for the next promise? It's even bigger (*and better*)!

Expect Your Moses Moment

You don't have to just hope for your Moses moment, my friends, you can *expect* your Moses moment, because He is a faithful and good Father!

Sometimes I wish that I could travel back in time and witness those moments in the story of the parting of the Red Sea just before the miracle. The palpable tension in the air as Moses stood on the edge of the water along with the thousands, or millions, of people that looked to him for leadership. The Bible says that the Israelites shook with fear and panic, expressing anger and hostility towards God and Moses because they felt trapped in this place of hopeless defeat. And yet, here's Moses, absolutely unshaken in His faith that God would make a way.

"Don't be afraid. Just stand still and watch the Lord rescue you today. The Egyptians you see today will never be seen again. The Lord himself will fight for you. Just stay calm." (Exodus 14:13-14 NLT)

You see, Moses did not just **hope** that God would provide a way. He **knew** He would. He expected it. Because He knew what a faithful Father we serve.

But not just Moses… let's hop over to the story of David and Goliath.

While the entire army of Israelites stood shaking in fear over one man, granted he was one very large and very strong man, just listen to David's confident words to King Saul…

"Don't worry about this Philistine, I'll go fight him!! … The Lord who rescued me from the claws of the lion and the bear will rescue me from this Philistine!" (1 Samuel 17:32,37 NLT)

Then, he spoke to Goliath…

"Today the Lord will conquer you…" (1 Samuel 17:46 NLT)

Think those are just the words of an overly self-assured young man puffing his chest before battle? No way! David was absolutely confident that the Lord would deliver.

The truth is, I wish I had that kind of confidence with my giants, with my healing, and with my hope for things that God has promised me. But I often find myself looping back to the anxiety and fear-filled question of *"But, how, God? How? I just don't see it."*

And here is what He keeps patiently and lovingly reminding me...

When our Heavenly Father gives us a promise, we aren't always provided with the details, the how or the when, but one thing is always certain... He *always* delivers.

He delivered that day for Moses.

He delivered that day for David.

He *will* deliver for me.

And He *will* deliver for you.

Do not let your confidence rest in what you can see and understand, but rather, in what an amazing, loving, and faithful Father you serve.

Even if you cannot see the path, *expect* that He will make the way.

Do not let your confidence rest in what you can see and understand, but rather, in what an amazing, loving, and faithful Father you serve.

Expect your Moses moment. Expect your David moment. Expect *your* moment. Because what He has promised, He will be faithful to deliver.

I encourage you to write a statement of confidence over whatever you are facing. Even if you don't fully believe it, write it and pray over it. Allow God to move through it. Allow Him to show you that you can rest in Him. He will fight for you. He will make a way.

He is the God of miracles.

The God who makes the unbelievable believable.

The God of paradigm shifts.

The God who delivers.

…

I'd like to conclude this chapter with some additional verses in hopes that they encourage your heart today…

Against all odds, when it looked hopeless, Abraham believed the promise and expected God to fulfill it. He took God at His word. (Romans 4:18 TPT)

"When Yahweh delights in how you live your life, he establishes your every step." (Psalm 37:23 TPT)

"I am the Lord, who opened a way through the waters, making a dry path through the sea…. But forget all that— it is nothing compared to what I am going to do.

For I am about to do something new. See, I have already begun! Do you not see it? I will make a pathway through the wilderness. I will create rivers in the dry wasteland." (Isaiah 43:16, 18-19 NLT)

He will make a path for you. Through your wilderness or out of your desert, He *will* make a way.

"When you go through deep waters, I will be with you. When you go through rivers of difficulty, you will not drown. When you walk through the fire of oppression, you will not be burned up; the flames will not consume you." (Isaiah 43:1-2 NLT)

"But those who trust in the Lord will find new strength. They will soar high on wings like eagles. They will run and not grow weary. They will walk and not faint." (Isaiah 40:31 NLT)

And I'm going to end this chapter with the same verse that we started it with, my friends, because I believe so much in the power of His promises…

For the authority of her faith rested in the One who made the promise, and she tapped into his faithfulness.

(Hebrews 11:11 TPT)

Chapter 6

When Feelings Threaten
Your Healing

I feel small and find myself taking up less space.

I am much less colorful than I once was and I fear that
I will never find joy again.

My light and spark have dimmed and sometimes I am
afraid that I will be swallowed up entirely.

I feel defeated and tired.

I feel hopeless.

I feel anxious.

I feel misunderstood.

I feel alone.

*And I find myself totally at the mercy of these feelings.
A lot.*

Does any of that sound familiar to you? I can recall a very vivid memory of how all of these emotions could, and would, come together in one unexpected moment and completely change my entire day:

It was the weekend and our family had decided to spend the day running errands together. The weather was beautiful and I felt happy and carefree. Suddenly a painful memory flashed through my mind. It was just a momentary thought, a split-second feeling, but I felt the familiar squeeze in my chest because I knew what was coming next and I was completely powerless to stop it.

I felt the sadness, anxiety, and fear begin to build. As it grew, I knew that it was only a matter of time before it swallowed me whole and I would be consumed by it for hours, possibly even days.

The panic began to rise and my heart desperately searched for somewhere to hide. I didn't want to be in this cycle of pain, anxiety, fear, and shame... I didn't! But I can't stop it. And somewhere deep inside, I knew that I would eventually stop fighting it altogether.

I would accept that life had changed me and I would always be this smaller, less colorful, and less joyful version of myself. The end.

Except God said... *"Not the end. You were crafted by my hands. Your very being has my fingerprint on it. You are exquisite and beautiful and covered in grace. I love you. Let me show you my heart."*

This topic is pretty heavy and I think it's very important that I share my heart right up front. There is no underlying message of shame here. There is no judgment over your feelings or your processing of those feelings. Do not let the enemy place that thought into this moment.

I'll say it again, although I have faced seasons that left me defeated, deeply injured, and scarred, I have not walked in your shoes. I do not pretend to know your pain. I cannot imagine the scars that have been carved deep into your heart or the incredible soul-crushing seasons that you have traveled through to get here.

But I can imagine someone telling that same girl above (*me*) that she is not chained to her feelings, that they do not have the power to control her day, and friends...

I can guarantee you that she would have told them that she has been so deeply defined by her painful seasons that she can no longer have an identity that is not tied to the resulting anxiety and fear. That she feels completely powerless to take the wheel and she's just along for the ride. And any guidance or response that suggested otherwise had to be coming from a place of judgment and deep misunderstanding.

But, how about you?

What feelings have been branded into your identity?

What feelings do you find yourself powerless to escape? Fear… anxiety… anger? In Chapter four, we worked on sifting through the words that have been written on our hearts as we allowed Him to begin the work of redefining us with His truths. But, what about the *feelings* that attempt to label us or brand us a certain way? Because He cares about those too.

Feelings simply do not obey our command.

Am I right?

I cannot *will* myself to feel something. I cannot force the hurt, sadness, anxiety, or anger away. I can compartmentalize, but in my experience this is really just reserving the feelings for later anyway.

So why can't we actually *control* our feelings? Because they are a natural and very genuine extension of the heart. They are a flashing signal to our brain that says, *"Hey… pay attention to me! There's something here. Something that brings joy or something that hurts."* And there is absolutely no shame in that.

Yes, feelings are a completely natural response to our life experiences and seasons, but may I share a personal and humble observation?

They can also become huge spiritual battlegrounds.

"Stay alert! Watch out for your great enemy, the devil. He prowls around like a roaring lion, looking for someone to devour." (1 Peter 5:8 NLT)

As we start this journey together, it's important that we take time to solidly lay the groundwork for the road ahead and I cannot stress this important note enough:

The enemy will use whatever tool he can to make you feel completely defeated, even very natural and completely understandable waves of feelings and emotions.

You see, when you are facing overwhelming and powerful feelings, he will whisper damaging thoughts into your ear and tell you that *you are forever lost in this abyss.*

And make no mistake, *that's exactly where he wants you.*

He took my cycle, my intense waves of emotions, and tried to convince me that I would *never* find my way out. That I was forever trapped, forever enslaved, forever chained to this life of defeat. And I almost believed him. *Almost.*

But why did he care? Because he will do *whatever* he can to get you to give up on this journey of healing.

He will take your pain, your difficult season, and he will attempt to create a huge spiritual battleground that you feel helpless and powerless to overcome; a barrier to your joy that feels too cluttered to find your way through. And if you're feeling that way today, this chapter is for you. Because even if you feel defeated in this moment, drowned out, pushed down, and swallowed up by your intense waves of emotions and feelings, I want you to hear this…

I know it may not feel like it right now, but you *are seen. Your feelings are understood. You are not alone. There is NOT something wrong with you. And most importantly, there is hope. You are not* chained to these emotions and powerless to take back control.

Hear this: He, the enemy, does not have the power to steal your promise of healing. You are not a product, the sum total of, or at the mercy of the remnants from your difficult seasons. You *will* overcome.

So, when you feel those intense emotions rising, that familiar tap on your heart and the wave of thoughts and feelings that follow, I encourage you to pause for a moment and ask yourself the roots...

Am I feeling a very natural emotion that comes with my processing of a difficult season or is this the enemy trying to pull me under again?

If you have traveled a difficult season, allow yourself the time and space to process. If you need extra help, seek out a professional counselor or therapist. (*I did this too*!)

Hurt and grief give rise to many emotions that should be recognized and given the love and grace to be worked through, not pushed aside. And the process is a journey. It should not be rushed or compared. We all travel through it differently. But I promise you, if you cling to Him, there is life on the other side and He will be faithful to get you there.

In the meantime, be intentional about guarding your thoughts and your heart. The enemy will use your process to try to drag you under, over and over, until you feel completely consumed and defeated.

If the enemy is turning your feelings into a painful spiritual battleground, threatening your healing and growth and leaving you defeated, I encourage you to speak victory over his lies.

Face this battle head-on. Choose to push relentlessly towards God's promise of healing and joy and draw strength from His presence to see you through. Stand firm over the enemy, even if it's in shaking courage. It may feel uncomfortable or unfruitful at first, but keep pressing in.

And if you need some steps of encouragement to follow, an additional road map to help you through those overwhelming moments of crashing waves, here are some things that I found very helpful in my own journey:

1. Pray. Even if you don't know what words to use, God knows your heart.

2. Pause to remember that your thoughts absolutely have the power to bear fruit, good or bad. If you hold onto the thought... *if you water it...* it will take root in your heart.

Draw strength from Jesus when you find yourself starting to spiral down that cycle. When I sat in the truck that day, it all started with one thought. That's all it takes. One thought... watered... is all the enemy needs.

3. Step into your authority over the enemy.

He has no power in our lives. Once we begin to recognize his lies and his games, we can tell him to flee and he has no choice. We don't need to reason with him, argue with him, or beg him for anything. Remember, God has given us ALL the authority over the enemy. When he tries to whisper lies of defeat and hopelessness, messages like, *"you're not good enough. You just don't get it. This healing isn't for you,"* turn to him and simply say, *"Leave."* Say it out loud, if needed... I know I did a few times.

And if you are feeling too defeated or weak in that moment, really struggling to take back your authority, have someone pray over you. Send a text to a friend and ask them to cover you in prayer. I did that too. Whatever it takes...

4. Remind yourself that you are not defined, labeled, branded, or controlled by your feelings. *You are not at their mercy, helpless to be swallowed whole.*

They are signals of something that makes your heart take pause. Believe me, I know from experience that they are often an extension of very real, and sometimes very raw, pain. They may go very deep, and they may feel incredibly overwhelming at times, but they are not *who* you are. Begin to believe and find strength in the identity that your Heavenly Father has been pouring into you and nothing more.

5. Find hope in His promises. This will give you HUGE victories.

   You see, as you put these steps into practice, you may see change OR it may feel really, really fruitless. That's how I felt at first. And God said, *"Rest, Shannon. Rest in my promises. You will feel joy again."*

   Today may not feel better. Tomorrow may not feel better either. Next week may feel like an even bigger battleground. But keep pushing through with hope and faith in His promises. We serve a Father that is loving and good and faithful and He will not let you fail.

As we know all too well, life is a series of seasons. We take delight in beautiful seasons of sunshine and happiness, but we will also face very difficult seasons filled with hardships, pain, and struggles. Happiness itself is not always possible and when joy is defined by our season in life or our momentary feelings, it will most definitely be squelched by the storms we will undoubtedly face.

Instead of anchoring our joy to a season of happiness, or a feeling, we can aspire to be intentional in all seasons. What does this mean? It means that, once again, joy does not come passively. It means that even in our darkest seasons, when it's the easiest to become bitter, angry and resentful, hopeless and defeated, we can still choose to be intentional with our thoughts, our heart, our words, and our actions.

Understand, there is nothing simple or perfect about this and it doesn't mean you have to be superhuman. It's a process and I often find that I have to re-evaluate where I am and re-align with where I'm going. Thank you, Jesus, for your grace!! After all, we are human and pain can make us feel all kinds of other emotions. But if we choose to be intentional, we are choosing to regularly stop, rest, evaluate, refocus, and trust Jesus to help with the rest.

Take a moment today to think about what it means to you to "be intentional." In both the good seasons and the difficult, we have the opportunity to evaluate the feelings with which we are renting space to in our hearts.

And when we do this, sometimes we discover things we don't like and we have to serve an eviction notice. Later, we may re-evaluate and have to serve another one to the same tenant. That's okay. That's growth. And it's beautiful. Give yourself credit for taking that step, even if it's over and over, and give yourself grace in the process. Because the more we practice, the easier it will become.

Ask yourself regularly if the feelings that you are

embracing and entertaining have become spiritual battlegrounds. And if so, take them to Him. Ask Jesus to be there with you *in the growth*, reminding you where He's taking you, and lifting you out of the defeating cycle of the enemies' attacks. Let Him remind you who you are in Him.

Fill your thoughts with my words until they penetrate deep into your spirit. Then, as you unwrap my words, they will impart true life and radiant health into the very core of your being. So above all else, guard the affections of your heart, for they affect all that you are. Pay attention to the welfare of your innermost being, for from there flows the wellspring of life. (Proverbs 4:21-23 TPT)

Additional Note: As I have learned in my own journey, the emotion of anger can be completely healthy. It's a natural feeling or reaction to being hurt or even afraid. There is no shame or judgment being placed here on the feeling or emotion of anger. When I speak of anger in this chapter, it is to warn against allowing that anger to move beyond the healthy and into the deep core of your spirit and your heart, giving it power to define who you are.

You see, the enemy will try to use your anger as a door and he will plant and water seeds of destruction. He loves to use anger because it's so easy to feel justified in our thoughts, words, and actions. If I can encourage you, take your anger to God. He can handle it. He will love you through the processing and the healing of it.

Chapter 7

Asking God to Use You

I am so excited about this chapter! In truth, I am absolutely on fire about this incredible and beautiful gift of the journey! I'm dancing in His presence as I share this message with you today. I believe in it so much! Are you ready for it?! Hold tight because if you really let it sink in, you may just feel your feet begin to move to the beat of the Kingdom's drums without so much as a warning! God is so good!

My friends, you are never too ordinary (*or too imperfect*) to make BIG moves for His Kingdom. Believe today that God is already using you and let that truth absolutely fill your heart with joy.

Can I tell you a story about a young girl that worked at a popular fast-food restaurant in a small East Texas town? She was a delightful young woman, but I'm sure she felt that her job taking orders was probably underwhelming and not particularly fulfilling. To this day, she has no idea the HUGE impact she had on me when God used her in that drive-thru lane. The way that

He poured over me when she simply said, "*Have a blessed day.*" The way that by simply carrying His presence with her, she was used by Him to touch my broken heart. The way that I needed that touch deep down because I had been traveling through a really difficult season and some days, like that day, I found myself trudging through the hard as part of my healing. I still regret not sharing with her the incredible impact that it had on me.

Or... Can I share with you the story of a physician assistant who found himself building wood crosses as a hobby after losing his mom to cancer? Building those crosses became a way that he connected with God and felt His healing touch move through a very shattered and shaken heart. One completely random day, he took an imperfect cross to his clinic job with the intention of selling it for just enough 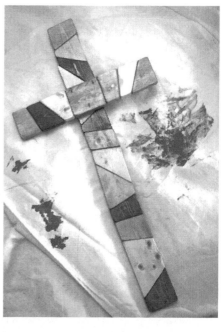 to cover the cost of materials. He couldn't have known as he packed it in his truck that morning how God was about to use his hobby and his heart in a very special and beautiful way.

That afternoon, a patient walked in and began to share her heartbreaking story about the devastating loss of her son. After a few minutes together, the PA felt God's nudge, His gentle press, and he excused himself to retrieve the cross from his desk. When he came back in the room, he stumbled his way through an explanation that he felt that this cross was meant for her. And a month later, he received a letter...

Five years after the loss of her son, she wrote that she felt God's peace entering her heart when she brought that cross home. Five years after an unimaginable loss, she began to feel His presence soothing her pain.

Little moves, my friends. Little moves with very powerful impacts!

I'll say it again... *you are never too ordinary (or too imperfect) to make BIG moves for the Kingdom.*

God doesn't see you as small. You are not insignificant, unimportant, insufficient, unskilled, or underwhelming. You are perfectly equipped, the exact fit, and divinely called. And your role in His Kingdom is *irreplaceable.*

He goes before you to prepare a way. He works within you to prepare your heart for His calling. And He walks beside you to light your path and guide your steps.

One of the most powerful prayers that I have ever spoken started with just four simple words... *"God, please use me."*

You see, earlier last year, I had just accepted a new role as a college instructor. I worried endlessly. Have I built a good curriculum? What would my students think of me? What would my new boss say? And well, you get the picture. One day, I decided to change my focus and try something new. Instead of my usual worries, I simply whispered, *"God, please use me. You know their needs. You know their hearts. Help me to touch them with your love. Let me be a light that exemplifies your goodness, your love, and your grace."*

It probably wasn't that beautiful when I stumbled my way through the prayer, but He must have known my heart because over the next several months, God used me in ways that I cannot even explain. He used me in ways that I don't even fully understand. But the joy it brought me to be a light for Him was simply indescribable.

As I reflect back on this experience, I am reminded of a lesson that I learned early on in my journey...

Being used by God is not always defined by the big, miraculous, and dramatic moves. *We do not have to be used in dramatic ways to have a dramatic, life-changing impact.* We each play an important and irreplaceable role in the Kingdom and joined together in our gifts, we become an unstoppable force!

It's not always the healing of the sick, parting of the waters, and slaying of the giants. Sometimes, it's just carrying His spirit within you and being willing to be used by Him in the little moments that sit between someone you touch and our Heavenly Father, often unseen and unwitnessed by anyone else. It's allowing Him to pour over them through you. And in all its simplicity, it is truly life-changing.

But I'm going to pause right here for a moment because I hear your heart asking that same familiar (*and painful*) question:

But, Shannon... Who am I? I am nothing special. Who am I to make big moves for His kingdom? Who am I to be used in ways that truly matter?

I'll be the first to tell you how broken I really am (*but Jesus!*). I'll be the first to admit how small I felt in the Kingdom; to tell you that I was just this small-town country girl, ordinary and underwhelming. Perhaps that's why I found such encouragement in the story of Moses. Because when God came to Moses and called him to free the children of Egypt, the very first question that Moses asked was...

But God, *"Who am I?"* (Exodus 3:11 NLT)

...And then he spent the next 40 years being radically and gloriously used by God over and over. Let that sink in for a moment.

Who am I?

Exactly who He needs.

Not small. Not underwhelming. Not insignificant. Not insufficient. EXACTLY who He needs.

Sometimes, it's just carrying His spirit within you and being willing to be used by Him in the little moments that sit between someone you touch and our Heavenly Father, often unseen and unwitnessed by anyone else.

Believe that He's already using you. Eagerly wait for His nudges and lean into them with a willing heart. Allow Him to pour through you, even in the mundane. And let your cup be filled with joy as you watch Him use you to touch others.

Live fully alive. Live with a heart to pursue His calling on your heart daily. And as you rise from the difficult, delight in how He uses you to lift others!

Today, I encourage you to simply ask God to use you. It may be with the cashier at the grocery store. It may be with the random person you meet on the sidewalk. It may be with your own family member or a friend. But watch and listen for His answer and lean in. The joy it brings to you, the vessel, will be indescribable. The tangible presence of the Holy Spirit as you carry Him within you will be undeniable. And you, my friend, will be blessed.

Chapter 8

A Pause For Extra

Ever notice how there are just some days when your children need a little *extra*? You know what I mean… An extra hug. An extra kiss. An extra "I love you." An extra pause where you just hold them and reassure them that they are safe and that they matter. And then, when their cup is full again, they launch back out into the world, ready for another adventure.

That is what your Heavenly Father wants to do for you today. He wants to give you, His child, a little "*extra.*"

As we have been walking through this journey together, He has been speaking to your heart so much. The journey has not always been a lighthearted dance. Not at all. At times, the weight of what we are carrying has increased because we are looking directly at it. We know that He is walking us towards healing, but we also know that before we can get there, we have to walk through "that" and it's a thought we push away whenever possible. We feel Him urging us on, but we are scared and honestly, reluctant.

Can I share something with you today?

It's going to be okay.

God is saying to us right now, *"Hit the pause button. Feel the pain. Let it pour over you and release it. Don't push it away. There is no healing in pushing it down. Allow yourself to grieve. And when you have finished, I will give you the strength to get up again and keep moving forward. It's only a pause. It's not the end."*

My beautiful friend, when the fear, anxiety, or doubt threaten your journey, please don't turn back. Don't run from it. Just hit the pause button. Let Him hold you through it. And tomorrow, we can lean in again... *together.* And we can repeat this process, together, as long as it takes to heal. He is with us and His promises are where we can safely anchor our hope.

You are His daughter and He knows your heart. He knows the fear. He knows the sadness. He knows the weight of it and how it holds you back. He knows. And sometimes, He is calling us to simply rest. No work. No action. Just rest. An extra moment where we let Him hold us through it.

If you need that today, I encourage you to lean into it and let Him pour over you. And then, revisit this chapter as many times as you need on the journey. Hit that pause button for a little extra.

Chapter 9

Pray For One Another

We know that God is omniscient, yet time after time, He calls on us to act as intercessory spiritual soldiers for each other. So, it begs the natural question... why? Why does God call on us to be a prayer warrior for others when He can literally bring Heaven to Earth without any "action" on our part?

After much thought and prayer over this question, I have come to this humble conclusion...

He asks because it brings us into a closer relationship with Him. Because it demonstrates our trust in Him and His will. Because it softens our hearts and grows our faith. Because it stirs a transformation in us from the inside out and allows the Holy Spirit to move in our lives. Because it brings us into God's presence, where we can witness His immense love and His unwavering faithfulness. And friends, that's just what it does for us. What about the person that we are lifting up in our prayers?

Sometimes we are asked to stand in the gap and seek our Heavenly Father's help, asking Him to pour out peace, comfort, clarity, joy, and grace over one another. Not because He wouldn't do it without our interceding, but simply because He delights in His children seeking Him together and praying over each other.

Other times, our prayer may serve as extra protection during a spiritual battle. Imagine literally taking up arms and standing in between the enemy and his target. When we pray, we are embracing our authority in Jesus Christ and saying to the enemy, "*You have no power here.*" Now imagine doing that for someone you love. Someone who is tired, defeated, and battle worn. You commit to being a prayer warrior for them. You have joined the fight. And not by your own power, but by the blood of Jesus and the authority given to you in His name, the enemy retreats.

Jesus loves when we stand in the gap for each other. And the more we do it, the more we will feel called to cover not only loved ones, but even strangers.

For though we live in the world, we do not wage war as the world does. The weapons we fight with are not the weapons of the world. On the contrary, they have divine power to demolish strongholds. (2 Corinthians 10:3-4 NIV)

All that said, I am going to pause for a moment and admit something right here. I spent many (*many*) years paying little or no attention to my prayer game. I honestly felt like God was going to do... well... whatever He wanted to do, with or *without* my prayers. Wow... that's a lot of honesty. But maybe you find it relatable?

All of that changed about a year ago. If you've ever been through a life circumstance that literally dropped you to your knees, then you likely understand the complete paradigm shift that took place in my heart when I witnessed the truly divine power of prayer. Let me explain...

Right in the middle of that overwhelmingly painful season, I had a beautiful friend reach out to me and express that God had been placing me in her thoughts and on her heart and she was praying for me. *What?* God wanted someone to pray for me? But why? Couldn't He just reach in and pull me out of the storm himself? I couldn't understand it.

Then, my Heavenly Father began to tap on my heart. He began to guide me in my own prayers. But *why?* Clearly He was seeing the pain and destruction. Couldn't He just whisper the cure to my situation and it be done? And yet, every time He met me, I was given a gentle push here or a soft nudge there; an answer that looked more like guidance and direction than the earth-shattering and pain-ending miracles that I so desperately sought.

What transpired over the next twelve months was a series of beautiful and sometimes very difficult conversations between my Heavenly Father and me.

I learned how much He loves me.

I learned that He created me and delights in me.

I learned that I am not here by chance, but that He has a calling on my heart.

I also learned that I can trust Him, even when the answer is *not* what I wanted.

I learned that He is there, even when I *feel* alone.

I learned that He can reweave my broken seasons and bring forth something beautiful from them.

And I learned how to give Him all of me and allow Him to guide my path.

Truly life-changing revelations. *NOT* something that I merely repeated robotically, like I did before. No, these became deeply rooted beliefs based entirely on the personal conversations that occurred between my heart and His.

There are many, many reasons why prayer is so very important, but I would like to share with you the biggest lesson that I learned in that year…

Prayer is our pathway to a *relationship* with Jesus. And that relationship is our link to peace, hope, encouragement, love, rest, and even joy in the middle of the raging storms or the difficult seasons we face.

Prayer is our pathway to a relationship with Jesus. And that relationship is our link to peace, hope, encouragement, love, rest and even joy in the middle of the raging storms or the difficult seasons we face.

I no longer see prayer as a way to ask for help from a God that I really don't know or understand. I see prayer as a conversation between my best friend and me. I await His response with no doubt in my heart that He will answer. And even if the answer is not what I had hoped, I have learned that there are just as many blessings in His "*no*" as there are in His "*yes*." But more importantly, I value my relationship with Him and I desire to be close to His heart.

Once I understood and truly respected the power of prayer, I started paying attention to how many times that I would tell a friend, "*I'll pray for you*," or "*I'll keep you in my prayers*." These may have been flippant words before (*ouch!*), but now I took them very seriously. I began to cover my friends and family in prayer, standing in the gap and asking God to pour over them in supernatural and divine ways that only He could. And in the process, I felt my life and my heart being completely transformed.

So today, I hope that you will join me in lifting each other up, in covering each other with prayer; carrying "*it*" together and fighting the battle side by side. And then, I hope Jesus just absolutely pours over you today. I hope you feel the many prayers that are being spoken for you. I hope you feel your Heavenly Father moving in your life. And I hope it brings you joy!!

Pray for courage. Pray for peace. Pray for clarity. Pray for comfort. Pray for strength. Pray for healing. And... Pray for joy.

Pray for every person that reads this book! Pray for those that came before you and those that will come after.

We are not only lifting each other up. We are carrying each other's burdens. We are taking up arms and fighting the spiritual battle alongside each other. We may not know each other, but our prayers will reach the ears of our Heavenly Father and He knows every hair on our head and every plea of our heart.

I believe wholeheartedly that we will witness God moving. I believe that we will see and feel His incredible touches all throughout this process; that His goodness and His power will be shaking the very ground that we walk on.

Today, my friends, we are standing in the gap for each other!

Chapter 10

The Path to Forgiveness

A dear friend of mine dropped me a text. In it she wrote, "*I think my next step of healing is to write an I forgive you list…*" I could not believe the timing of her message. It was the exact topic that I had felt led to write about today. Could it be because God is tapping on all of our hearts and saying, "*I cannot pour My fullness of joy into the same cup as deep resentment, bitterness, and unforgiveness*"? Like adding lemon juice to a cup of hot milk, they just don't mix without creating a lumpy, curdled mess.

Forgiveness seems to be a constant topic between me and God. I knew deep down that we had to clean up the mess, but it didn't stop me from searching for another rabbit hole that we could go down instead. What is it about unforgiveness that is sometimes so difficult to face?

Each time I would find myself resisting, He would patiently and gently put the message on repeat for as long as needed and lovingly reassure me that He had prepared me and that He would be with me. Until eventually, I conceded.

Okay, we will try this, God, but no promises. I'm not very good at forgiveness, as you know.

As we started the process, some forgiveness came rather easy. Old hurts. Random clutter that I had held onto in my heart. I gained traction with each step and as I found the weight lifting, I also gained confidence. I was digging through my unforgiveness like a junk drawer.

"This can go…" and I would toss it in the trash.

"This one too…"

…until I actually found myself laughing at my own stubbornness. Why did I resist this so much? I can do this! Look at me go! I'm so proud of myself.

And then God reached *"that"* one… and I paused.

I looked at it and I felt Him urge me forward.

"Yes, that one," He gently pressed.

And I closed the drawer.

I kid you not. I closed the drawer.

I'll clean *"that"* one out another day, I resolved, promising Him that we would loop back when I felt stronger and more able.

The truth is, I didn't know how to clean that one out. And, while we are being honest, there was a time that I didn't think that I should *have* to clean that one out. I could absolutely justify that unforgiveness. A jury would most definitely find me not-guilty of improper harboring of resentment and anger... I was sure of it. *But still, God pressed.*

Why? Because they don't mix. We know it and He knows it. The two just don't mix. I could not chase joy and simultaneously harbor such deep and soul-crushing unforgiveness.

Can I share a personal story with you for a minute? Last year, my father experienced some pressing chest pain and my mom decided to take him to the ER. What they found was a buildup of plaque in one of his arteries that was restricting the blood flow to his heart. The doctors said he was lucky because the blockage had been caught early. Left untreated, it would completely block *all* blood flow to his heart.

Yes, I'm pausing right along with you to let that fully sink in. Left untreated, unforgiveness and resentment restrict the blood flow to our hearts and have the potential to form painful and life-threatening blockages.

He's nudging our spirits right now. He's teaching us why forgiveness is so very important. Even when it's really, really hard. *Especially* when it's really, really hard.

The journey does not promise to be easy. Sometimes

I feel like that leftover junk in my drawer is easier to avoid than heal. The scar simply runs too deep and my anger and resentment will not be overcome painlessly. And although I know that my life will be better after treatment, I often find myself questioning if I really want to go through the discomfort of removing and healing this restricting blockage?

But if I dig deep down, the answer becomes simple and crystal clear to me. Yes, I do. Because I am reminded of the promises of my Heavenly Father and I know that if I simply follow His lead, I will find myself on different ground. He will replace my running shoes with dancing shoes and I *will* dance with joy again.

I do not know what the first step to forgiveness will look like for you, but may I share a few of my favorite insights that I have picked up along the way...

The Decision to Forgive

When I made the decision to forgive, one could argue that there was no actual change that took place in that moment at all... *except there was.* Because I had made an expressed agreement between my head, my heart, and God that we were going to stop ignoring this festering wound and begin to take steps forward in healing.

You see, that festering wound was leaking. I knew it and He knew it. It leaked onto those that I loved the most. It leaked onto the innocent: my son, my family, my friends, and even complete strangers. And while I wanted so badly to contain it, the truth is that a festering wound left untreated spreads. And it was time to bring this deep, seeping infection to the One True Healer before it damaged even more.

But that *decision to forgive* didn't remove the fact that there were still times when my anger and pain roared. It didn't spontaneously cure the resentment and heal my heart. It didn't even truly change the fact that I still felt completely justified in holding onto it, *all* of it. No, in truth, there was no instantaneous change in me that could be documented whatsoever. It was simply and beautifully an expressed agreement between my heart and God that, deep down, I knew it was time to surrender; I knew it was time to lay it all at His feet.

You see, the forgiveness that He was encouraging me to walk through was more about me than them. The unforgiveness that I was harboring in my heart had allowed this infection, and the resulting pain and anger, to grow so grossly oversized that it was killing me from the inside out. Killing my spirit. Killing my joy. And worse, it was killing those that I loved the most. Yes, it was time to make the decision to face my junk drawer and *all* its contents once and for all.

Forgiveness is a Journey

But can we talk about the journey of forgiveness for a moment? Because so many of the messages that we hear about it, especially as believers, create this expectation of some grand David-and-Goliath moment where we swiftly and confidently defeat our giant of unforgiveness with one single, powerful blow. And honestly, this expectation left me more defeated than my giant.

I want to encourage your heart for a moment. It's okay if your process of forgiveness does not feel like a one-and-done earth-shattering David-and-Goliath moment. The truth is, true and deep forgiveness, the kind that comes from His healing touch and is rooted in His divine peace, is rarely so swift. Here's why...

Unforgiveness is often deeply rooted in a moment of life-shattering pain. The kind of pain that drops you to your knees or leaves you in the fetal position on the floor. The kind of pain that steals your joy, your normalcy, your light, in one fast swoop. And that kind of pain gives rise to all kinds of feelings within us. Bitterness, anger, resentment, hopelessness, grief, depression, and more. These feelings need to be acknowledged by us and worked through with Him, not forced into submission, if we seek true, deep healing.

No, forgiveness is rarely (*if ever*) achieved wholly in one moment. It's often a decision made over and over, a process that we lean into and take back to Him as many times as it takes... *for as long as it takes*.

Forgiveness is a journey.

Give yourself grace along the way. There is no perfectly mapped out, tested and proven action plan that sets your course and makes forgiveness stumble-proof.

Yes, God can (*and did*) pour peace beyond understanding into my heart, but there were still days when I would trip over the same rock in my path and my unforgiveness would roar, yes ROAR, from within.

What? Where did that come from? I thought we had made more progress than that?

And sometimes I would place it at His feet only to find myself in another angry spiral of spirit-crushing thoughts, grief, and memories, and realize that I had picked it right back up, again… Why? *Because it hurt*!

Because it hurt in that really deep place that made me want to curl up and hide or throw something. Because anger, resentment, and sadness would wash over me. And because I felt justified. In fact, I *knew* I was justified in all of those feelings. There were moments when I would run through the reasons, defending my argument forwards and backwards with God on why I had every right to be angry, and I'd do it so fast that He couldn't get a single word in. And like the patient and loving Father that He is, He would stay and He would listen. But then, He would gently remind me….

Fix your eyes on where I am taking you. My child, you cannot take this with you. It will weigh you down on the journey, defeating your hope and your strength. The weight it carries is simply too much. The messages it whispers as you carry it will shatter your spirit and bind you to this place, unmoving. Let go. Let me heal it. Let me move through it. Trust me. Walk with me…and when you're ready, we will run… together!

You see, we can focus on all the reasons why we have every right to plant roots in this place of anger and resentment. Or, we can focus on where He's taking us and lean into that healing. But we can't do both.

We either plant roots or we pick up our feet into that next step.

This is not to say that the next step means we are healed. Remember, it's a process. But I am saying that I don't want to plant roots and live here. I'm tired, defeated, exhausted, and sad. And He's looking into my eyes and saying...

Trust me. Pick up your foot. Take one step forward, towards My voice, and make the decision today to walk with Me through this.

And if I might add: Sometimes in that moment, in that weighing of our options to either plant roots or move forward, the decision to forgive and the resulting journey through the process of forgiveness can feel completely unfair. Sometimes it feels so wrong that we have to do all this hard work because of the pain that someone else has caused. But when that thought, that feeling, threatens your progress, remember this:

It's worth it. Worth it for the healing and joy that He has in store. Worth it for the future that He is promising. Worth it because God is saying, "*This is not the end of your story. I will bring you through.*" And He will provide abundantly. All we have to do is take it to Him, over and over, and let Him work through it and within us.

Forgiveness Is Not About What We Can Do

There is one final (*and vitally important*) detail that I have learned in my forgiveness journey - one last note to remember when it comes to those days when it all feels just so very overwhelming - and it is this:

There is no shame in saying to Him that you feel incapable and unable to forgive. The truth is that He doesn't expect you to make the journey alone.

He doesn't expect us to depend on our own strength to conquer this giant. He didn't ask that of David and He won't ask that of you.

You see, there were times on my forgiveness journey when I felt so defeated. Am I ever going to rise above this? Or worse, *does this unforgiveness that I'm struggling with make me a terrible Christian?* Ouch. You see, that's often what the messages of *religion* would have us believe. That we have failed Him. That we are a terrible example of what He wants. That He can't even look at our unforgiveness, at our hearts, without utter disgust. But let me separate the messages rooted in the man-made aspects of *religion* and share something with you that I have learned in my deeply personal *relationship* with God...

He has never (*ever, ever*) made me feel that way. And He won't for you either.

He held me when I was angry. He wept with me when I broke. He patiently listened when I poured out my bitterness and told Him that I didn't want to forgive and in fact, I *shouldn't have to.* And then, He lovingly lifted me up each day and encouraged me to try again, all while pouring His love over me and reminding me that I was His treasured, cherished, and beautiful daughter, today and every day. *And that is the incredible Father we serve!*

And guess what… I'm still working with Him today on some of my unforgiveness. Gasp! Am I really writing a chapter in this book about forgiveness when I still have my own unforgiveness that He and I are working through? Yes, I am. Because it's time for us to be real and talk about His love and His grace. It's time for us to talk about true, deep, life-changing healing. Because it's a process, a journey, that may take bringing it back to Him over and over. And I've come to realize that's okay. In fact, it's better than okay! He is delighting in us simply making the decision to *start* the journey with Him!

And my friends, the key to what I'm saying is this…

While we *do* need to make the decision to clean out the junk drawer, we will *never* be doing it alone.

We have to make the choice to face the hard, the really, really hard. We have to place the blockage that is threatening our hearts in the hands of the One True Healer. And we have to expect that the journey will have moments that send us face-first to the ground. *When that happens, give yourself grace. There is no perfect formula and we are all learning in the process.*

But pause for a moment at any point and you'll hear your Heavenly Father reminding you that you are never alone, that you are never too broken or too weak, and that He will lovingly walk you through this, all the way through this, guiding you, carrying you at times, and healing you throughout.

Forgiveness does not depend on what *we* can do. It's all about what He can do within us. When we make the choice to lean into Him, He will begin the work within us and we will face the unforgiveness... *together*.

So, the next time that you find yourself deep in doubt wondering how you are going to do this, arguing that you don't have the strength or that you shouldn't have to carry this weight that someone else placed on you, pause and remember Who is with you and where He is taking you. You only need to draw close, draw strength and courage from His promises, and set it at His feet, as many times as it takes. He will meet you there because He is a good and faithful Father.

Chapter 11

The God Who Sees You

I have called you by your name; You are Mine.
(Isaiah 43:1 NKJV)

Dear friends, I want to share something so powerful and so very important with you right up front in this chapter…

You are not just one of many to our Heavenly Father, going unnoticed as you blend in with the masses, insignificant and small.

No, the One who loves you most knows your every joy and your every sorrow, your every fear and your every pain, your every hope and the things about which you dream the most. He knows every beautiful moment that took your breath away and every gut-wrenching season that left you gasping for breath.

He knew you first. Before you were born. Before you were conceived. And He has known you, truly known you, and loved you every day since. He delights in you.

You are His special treasure. His beautiful daughter. And He cares about you today.

"Lord, you know everything there is to know about me. You perceive every movement of my heart and soul, and you understand my every thought before it even enters my mind. You are so intimately aware of me, Lord. You read my heart like an open book and you know all the words I'm about to speak before I even start a sentence. You know every step I will take before my journey even begins. You've gone into my future to prepare the way and in kindness you follow behind me to spare me from the harm of my past. You have laid your hand on me! This is just too wonderful, deep, and incomprehensible! Your understanding of me brings wonder and strength…

You formed my innermost being, shaping my delicate inside and my intricate outside, and wove them all together in my mother's womb…

How thoroughly you know me, Lord! You saw who you created me to be before I became me! Before I'd ever seen the light of day, the number of days you planned for me were already recorded in your book. Every single moment you are thinking of me! How precious and wonderful to consider that you cherish me constantly in your every thought!"

(Psalm 139:1-6, 13, 14-18 TPT)

…

Few memories in my life compare to the day that God left me a very personal love note in the woods. It spoke so powerfully to my heart and left me in a mess of tears. It wasn't the note itself, but rather the realization He truly noticed and loved me... Simple, small, and seemingly insignificant me. And I found myself completely overwhelmed.

Overwhelmed by the thought that my *"little"* would even be on the radar of a Heavenly Father that must have so much *"big"* on His plate at all times.

Overwhelmed by the realization that I'm not just one of many, but that He truly sees me. He knows me. And He loves me that much.

Overwhelmed by the love of a Father that does not see the ninety-nine and simply forget about the one, because well, He already has so many, so why bother?! No, He sees the heart of each and every child. He sees me. And He sees you.

Later in this chapter, I'll share with you the full story of my adventure in the woods that led to that very special love note, but first I want to share with you a few incredible stories from people close to me that demonstrate exactly what we are talking about in this chapter. They are stories of a Father who sees us and cares about our hearts; stories that will leave you in tears as the realization truly sinks in... He treasures each one of us. We are known, *individually*, and we are loved, touched, spoken to, and poured over by Him in our own unique and beautiful ways.

From a dear friend:

One of my favorite "*God is in the details*" stories is from when I was in ministry school. I wasn't able to work. I had very little in my bank account, but I went to Target anyway.

While at Target, I found a sweater I loved and it was on sale. At that time, I thought it was going to be marked down even more when I got to the register – it wasn't. I took it home and balanced my checkbook and I knew I wouldn't be able to afford the gas I needed for the week, so I returned the sweater.

I was devastated. This sounds small and trivial, but I'm not a person that buys clothes or things for myself, and to have found something I loved only to return it because I couldn't afford it hurt my heart.

A week later, the daughter of my ministry school director gave me two bags of clothes from cleaning out her closet and in one of those bags was the sweater.

Not only did God give me the gift of that sweater back, but He gave me abundantly above all I could have imagined! I didn't need to worry about affording/buying any more clothes for the rest of that year. He gave me a totally complete wardrobe.

He really cares about the Big things and the small things.

- E

From another person close to my heart:

During a financially difficult season in my life, I really wanted a new Bible but I just couldn't afford one. I had a very specific Bible in mind that I had grown to love, the Spirit Filled Life Bible. Although I would have liked to just drive down to my local Christian bookstore and purchase it, budget-wise there just wasn't anything extra leftover each month to do so. So, I decided to pray and bring my heart's desire to God.

One day while driving, I came up to an intersection and there, in the middle of the road, was a book. A book... unexplainably just sitting in the middle of the road in front of me. So, I decided to jump out and take a look. It was a copy of the Spirit Filled Life Bible. No name inside its cover. No markings. The exact Bible that I had asked God to help me find a way to afford was sitting in the middle of the intersection that day.

- M

...

From a personal experience:

I made a new friend recently. A total God-placed moment led to our connection because much like me, she had recently traveled through a difficult season. When we finally let our guards down with each other and shared our hearts, we were able to lift each other just a bit in encouragement and hope.

When I left our conversation that night, God placed it on my heart to give her a very specific book that had been truly life-changing in my healing process. But there was one problem... My only copy was scribbled on and highlighted and messy.

I spent the next couple of weeks scouring local used bookstores, thrift shops, and even a Christian bookstore trying to find a copy of the book, but had zero success. I visited at least nine to ten stores and just couldn't find one single copy of this #1 bestseller.

Fast forward another week or two and I finally resolved to order the book online. When I looked up the price, I realized that I could only afford one copy. *Oh man*, I thought to myself, *I really wanted to order one for her and one to use in an upcoming book giveaway on my blog.* Knowing that I just couldn't squeeze the budget that tight, I finalized the order with just one copy in my cart.

It took a week for the book to come in and then another couple of days for me to pick it up at the post office (*rural area life*). Once I finally got it home, I set the book on the counter and just stared at it for a few minutes, an internal debate rising.

Do I use it for my blog? Or give it to this new friend? What if she thinks I'm weird? What if it hits too close to the heart because it's a book about healing? Or, what if I'm wrong? What if it's the opposite? What if it doesn't really speak to her at all? What if I look foolish and totally embarrass myself?

(*Friends, I still worry at times if I'm truly hearing Him correctly because when you feel vulnerable by what He's asking you to do, it can be a normal knee-jerk reaction to question if it's truly His voice that is calling you into that discomfort. But don't worry, if you ask Him, and lean into His voice and His answer, He will always let you know it's Him. Just watch what He does next...*)

In the end, I decided to play it safe. I would just use the book for my blog.

With that decision made, *and any possibility of discomfort on my end squelched*, I reached into my drawer and pulled out one of my "Pass Along Book" stickers. I use these stickers in book giveaways to encourage readers to pass along the book after they read it and pray for the next person in line. But just then, as I began to peel the sticker off the sheet, I felt God press on my heart... "*No, Shannon*"... and it was more than enough to make me pause, so I left the sticker sheet sitting on the counter while I debated what to do next.

I walked back and forth between that sticker sheet and folding laundry for the next 45 minutes. Finally, I decided to put the entire sheet of stickers back in the drawer and just ask the one question that already sat hanging unspoken in the air... "*God, what would you like me to do with this book?*" The answer was immediate and crystal clear. I once again felt His familiar nudge as He pressed her name on my heart.

Okay, God. I understand.

I quickly packaged the book in a small white gift bag, stapled the top so that nobody could peek, and decided I would drop it off at her work the next day. Satisfied that I had listened and followed His direction, I decided that a nice warm bath sounded like a perfect end to my night. But, just about the time that I had resolved myself to this plan, God quickly stepped into that thought and shook things up again...

"Tonight, Shannon. Take it tonight."

And so, I did. I loaded up our little guy and drove straight to her workplace to drop off the gift. And friends, that's where His plan became beautifully and perfectly clear to me, all of it. Because as she looked at the gift that we had just handed to her, she quietly whispered to the two of us...

"It's my birthday. And nobody knew."

And in that moment, I realized...

Nobody...but God.

He knew it all. He knew it was her birthday. He walked ahead of me to plan this moment. Every detail. Every coincidence. Every piece of the puzzle. Every disappointing trip to each and every bookstore. Every

103

delay. He was in it all. And as this truth continued to sink in, I found myself climbing into my truck with my eyes full of tears as well. He is so good.

…

So, why does a sweater, a Bible, a gift, and a love note in the woods matter so much? Because it's a beautiful demonstration of the fact that we are loved by a Heavenly Father that truly *sees* each one of us.

He sees our hearts.

He sees our pain and fear.

He sees our joy and hope.

He sees our dreams.

He sees our needs (both big and small).

He sees the things that we hide from the rest of the world.

He sees the icky that we work so hard to bury deep inside.

And He sees the treasure within us that is just waiting to be discovered.

He delights in knowing us, individually, and having a relationship with us where we can grow to know His heart just as He has always known ours.

In a world where it's easy to feel like one of many,

invisible, isolated, and alone, He is continually reminding us that *He is the God who sees*. He sees me. And He sees you.

When our troubles, our pain, and our trials feel insignificant or less important compared to the burdens of others, He says, "*Not to me. 'Your trivial' is not unimportant. It matters.*"

When the world seems to keep spinning around you and you feel completely unnoticed in your depression, your anxiety, or your hurt...

When you feel your heart crying out for someone to look over, to notice, and to scoop you up and hold you until the pain subsides...

When you find yourself wondering if you'll ever feel the sun's warmth again...

He is saying, "*I see you. I am here. And you are not small, insignificant, or alone. You are my child. And I care about your broken heart. Let me hold you. Let me heal you.*"

He is inviting us to rest in the truth that when we feel completely unseen or forgotten, we are never unnoticed by Him!

You see, God is not just the God of the big miracles and ground-shaking moves. He's the God of the little too. *And when we begin to see His touch in the little things, we begin to see His touch in everything.* We begin to realize that He cares about our mundane and our major. We begin to feel His heart pouring over our day, every day, as we journey through healing and as we seek joy in even the most difficult seasons.

So, the next time you feel unimportant or unnoticed, remember this …

Who is He?

The God Who Sees Me.

And He is the God Who Sees You.

You will not get lost in the crowd. He is there. Listen for the ways that He is speaking to your heart today and remember that you are deeply cherished by Him, always.

My Personal Story of God's Very Special Love Note in the Woods

Did you know that our Heavenly Father delights in sharing love notes with us all throughout the day? Little messages scattered in the details. Reflections of His love meant just for you (and me).

I had the most incredible personal experience with a love note from God one summer day. It was undeniably one of the most significant moments of my journey to-date and serves as a constant reminder that He cares about us, individually.

But before we start, I want to take a moment and share something right up front with you and it is this...

There's nothing extraordinarily special about me. I'm a very ordinary girl. But as ordinary as we may feel, God loves to show us how special we are *to Him.*

Some stories are just too good not to share. Here's mine...

During a recent visit to the grocery store, our son asked if I would buy him a pack of bathtub markers. I tried my best to redirect his attention to the wide selection of bubble bath options, but he just absolutely had his heart set on these markers. So, I gave in. When we brought them home, he couldn't wait to eat his dinner and jump right into the bath! For the next hour, he excitedly called us into the bathroom over and over to show off his newest masterpiece.

Well, evidently they were a good find because the markers quickly became a constant source of family entertainment. Everyone wanted to try them out and it wasn't long before I started to find fun little love notes all over our shower walls, messages left behind for the next beloved occupant. A heart (or twenty) here. An "I love you" there. Even smiley faces and flowers.

One morning, my son was taking a shower and he yelled, "Mommy, come look! Daddy left me a note in the shower." I pulled back the curtain and sure enough, while getting ready for work, my husband had left a note that read, "I love Ryan." I looked down at our little guy and he was beaming with pride and joy at the message left just for him on our shower wall.

Later that afternoon, as I was taking my shower, I glanced over to where the special message had been just a few hours earlier. Water had sprayed in that direction during my son's shower and all that remained were some red smears on the wall, but it was a beautiful reminder of a love note that touched the heart of one special little boy. As I sat in the pure joy of that memory, I heard my Heavenly Father suddenly speak into my heart, "*Watch for my love notes today,*" and friends, what transpired next completely changed my life.

If you will, allow me to pause here and give you some background before we move forward. You see, throughout most of that year, God had been teaching me so much about listening for His voice and learning to lean in. He had been a guiding hand through a very difficult season and the more that I learned to follow His direction and submit myself, the more that I found tremendous blessings in His lessons, even the hard ones. Not only had He been blanketing me in peace and grace, but He had also been stirring an indescribable fire inside me and I was falling in love with just sitting in His presence.

Having already experienced His incredible love and goodness all throughout my journey and having grown to delight in those moments when He fills my space, you can just imagine my excitement when He said, "*Watch for my love notes today.*" I quite literally couldn't wait! I knew that God had something really neat in store. But the truth is, I had no idea just how much I would learn about His heart that day and how it would profoundly change my relationship with Him forever.

Which loops me back to my story…

The plan for the afternoon had already been set. We were getting ready for a short out-and-back hike. Nothing exciting except that I had picked a spot that we had never explored and we were just going to follow the well-beaten trail and hope to find a wildflower field or a nice spot on the river to sit for a while. At first, the goal was simply to get out of the house for a few hours, but now I was especially eager to hit the road, and the trail, to see what God had in store. As my excitement built, I felt God interrupt my thoughts once again and remind me of a verse that He has so often been pressing on my heart…

"The Lord answered me: Write down the vision; write it clearly on clay tablets so whoever reads it can run to tell others. It is not yet time for the message to come true, but that time is coming soon; the message will come true. It may seem like a long time, but be patient and wait for it, because it will surely come; it will not be delayed." (Habakkuk 2:2-3 NCV)

Because I feel Him looping me back to that verse regularly, I have started making it a habit to document His words the moment that I hear His voice rather than waiting for the fruition of His promises. So, on that particular afternoon, I ran downstairs and quickly typed out what I had heard Him speak. I ended my short note with, *"Oooooo…. this should be fun!"*

On the way to the trailhead, I felt God urging me to share His message with our then five-year-old son. The conversation went something like this...

"Ryan, what do you know about God?"

That He loves us.

"How do you know that?"

Because you tell me.

"Well, did you know that God speaks to us? God told me today that He plans to leave us love notes to show us how much He loves us. Can you help me watch for them?"

Oh. Okay.

Soon after, he fell asleep and I drove the rest of the way to the trailhead deep in my own thoughts. *What kind of love notes would God leave?*

While unloading Ryan and our pup, Obi, at the trailhead, I paused for a moment to remind my little guy, *"Watch for God's love notes today and let me know if you see any."*

He happily agreed and off we went.

The first of the three love notes was hard to miss. We immediately noticed that the trail was almost littered with dozens of heart rocks. And, if you know me, you know I love *(love!)* heart rocks! But these heart rocks were insanely perfect and beautiful. They were amazing!

"Look, Ryan! So many heart rocks! God left us love notes!"

Oh...

I could feel his little brain turning as he chewed on this idea, deciding for himself if he believed it.

And then I felt God whisper... *there's more.*

Further down the hike, we took a little detour, a smaller side trail to the edge of a cliff. As we looked across the valley, I noticed that the pine tree we were standing next to had the shape of a heart carved out. It must have been there for some time because the tree had actually healed around it. Now, while I'm used to seeing carvings in aspen trees everywhere on a hike, it is very unusual to see a carving in a pine tree. In fact, in all my time hiking around our area, I had never seen something like this before.

"Look, Ryan! A heart in the tree! God left us another love note!"

My amazing little boy, a born leader and independent thinker, quickly replied quite matter-of-fact, *"But didn't someone else carve that heart in the tree?"*

"Yes, absolutely! But sometimes God guides us to places just to show us things."

I could tell he wasn't quite convinced, but my heart was truly enjoying this adventure and these conversations, opportunities to teach him about how much God loves us and how we are invited daily to have a personal *and very real* relationship with Him.

And then I felt God whisper… *there's more.*

So, I rallied my crew and we continued on.

After a while, I announced to my little group that we would be turning around soon because it was getting late and we needed to get back to the truck and head home before dark.

"Can I just climb this one big rock before we go back?" my son asked.

Of course.

So, I stood there as they climbed the rock from all different angles. Some worked. Others didn't. We laughed and took pictures. It had been a fun and beautiful day for a hike and my heart was absolutely full.

Then I heard God enter my thoughts once more…

There, He whispered as I looked past my son and into the woods.

"What?"

Walk there.

"In the woods?"

The thought of Him directing me into the woods felt strange, (*Am I hearing you right, God?*) but as soon as the doubt entered my head, I felt His familiar press again.

There.

About this time, you are likely thinking this story sounds very odd. Don't get me wrong, it was a very strange moment for me too. This entire hike we had not left the established trail – *not once* – and yet I clearly felt Him pressing me to walk straight into the woods, directly past the large rock that my son was climbing on.

I hesitated for a split second, but then I remembered something that shifted my entire line of thinking. You see, if I have learned nothing else in the past year, I have learned this:

It is in those moments when I have trusted His voice and obediently leaned in that I have learned the most about God's love for me.

So, I walked…

…in a straight line…

…directly past that large rock…

…into fairly dense woods…

…for about 40 yards…

...and quite literally walked straight to this...

Another Love Note From God!

Now, before you think this is truly an odd story about God's love, let me share with you why this love note was so incredibly significant and personal to me...

I have lived in Colorado for much of my life, but this year was my first experience with shed hunting. Shed hunting is when you search the woods for antlers that have been naturally shed by deer and elk over the very early spring months. There's a real art to it and although I did a lot of research and gave it my best shot, I struggled. At one point during a shed hunt, I caught myself asking God, "*Can you help me find one?*" And then I immediately felt ashamed. With all the important healing going on in my heart, much less the incredible needs of others, how could I be asking God to help me find shed antlers? How unimportant and trivial.

Fast forward to today, a random day (*yes*), but a day when God specifically told me to "*Watch for (His) love notes*" and here I found myself standing over the kind of find that I (personally) would *maybe* see once in a lifetime. This was not a shed antler... This was a fully intact 4×4 bull elk skull. I wish I could adequately express the level of excitement that I felt in that moment.

For a good long pause, this girl that has no shortage of topics to chat about at any time, any day, with anyone was left... completely speechless.

I know I've said it before, but I truly feel it's so important to say it again...

It was not the gift that was in front of me that made my heart leap the most. It was the overwhelming joy that came with the realization that this was a love note designed just for me. Me. He loves me so much that He gifted me something very specific, very personal, and very special.

But as I was about to realize, there were even more blessings in that gift than I had initially comprehended.

You see, once I found my bearings again, I turned to my son with the biggest smile. I truly didn't think the moment could get any better, but as my son smiled back at me, I heard him say with total delight, "God really *did* leave us love notes today!" And my eyes filled with tears.

Yes, He did, baby. Yes, He did.

You better bet that I hauled that skull back to the tree with the heart and took a picture of the two together. It now hangs in a special place in our home and serves as a daily reminder to our family that...

God is very real.

God cares about the little, as well as the big.

And God delights in showing us how much He loves us, daily.

It was an amazing story to share with my husband that evening when he beat us home and read the note on my computer. Love notes from a beautiful and very real Heavenly Father and a reminder for us all.

So why did this gift in the woods and these stories of a God who sees have such a profound, life-changing impact on my relationship with Jesus? Because it was not just any sweater. It was a very specific sweater. It was not just any Bible. It was a very specific Bible. A very specific ask. A very personal gift. Because it is proof of a very personal, loving, and beautiful God who sees us individually and cherishes us, pours over us, in our own unique ways. It's the incredible realization that we are known, truly known, by Him.

And one randomly glorious (not so random) day, I have full faith and confidence that it will be a very specific skirt, a long white flowing skirt with beautiful flowers, that will absolutely demonstrate the fulfillment of His promises to me at the beginning of this journey. But friends, I'll say it again...

There is nothing extraordinarily special or unique about me. The invitation is open to us all. Watch for His love notes. Watch for the way that He speaks to you... The unique, beautiful, and very *seen* you.

Don't dismiss His messages as coincidences or products of your imagination. He's there. In the small. In the big. In the details. In the mundane. He's there. And He delights in showing you His heart.

In a world where it's easy to feel like one of many, invisible, isolated, and alone, He is continually reminding us that He is the God who sees!

Chapter 12

Step Into Your Authority

Fear. Sometimes I feel like I've lived my whole life with my wheels spinning in place because of the constant life-restricting ebb and flow of my own worry-filled thoughts. They readily and regularly remind me of all the what-ifs and the unknowns.

Fear of how I will handle it. Fear that I will crumble. Fear that someone will hurt me. Fear that I won't be good enough. Fear that I am not strong enough. Fear that the next shoe is going to drop and I will be left shattered again. Fear that I will fail. Fear that I'll look foolish. *Fear that I'll never overcome this absolutely awful cycle of fear*.

I was going to start this chapter off with a funny story, one that always lightens the mood when I broach the topic of fear, but then I am gently reminded that fear has been a deep, painful, and very real part of my journey and I'm not being fully transparent and vulnerable when I joke about it and fail to truly acknowledge the deep scars that it once dug into my heart.

You see, every amazing opportunity, every new potential friend, every exciting career step, fresh start, and even the joy of a new adventure or new day was utterly smothered, at times, by fear. It invaded my every spark of hope, an uninvited trespasser, demanding I be more realistic with myself. And with time, I began to listen. I expected to fail, and worse, I expected others to fail me.

"If I step out, someone will definitely misunderstand me. Someone will unfairly judge me. Someone will call out the small person that I truly am and remind me that I don't belong at their table."

Fear.

What if I never overcome this absolutely awful cycle of fear?

If you find yourself relating to anything that I've said in this chapter so far, I wanted to take a moment and encourage your heart...

These next few pages will not be what you expect. In fact, it definitely wasn't what I expected. Because you see, I thought that in order to chase joy, and live life fully alive, I would have to face down my fears, once and for all, and walk away a winner; that I had to go to war and somehow find a way to defeat and overcome this huge, life-long struggle. And in truth, the mere thought of that burden left me defeated, effectively losing the battle, before we even got started.

But friends, that's not how it happened at all. And I can promise you… that's not what this chapter is all about.

Hang with me here and I'll explain what I mean because in my own journey, I discovered that the remedy for this lifelong stumbling block was far less complex and much more beautiful than I ever understood or anticipated!

But first, let me pause and share with you some of the fears that regularly challenged my growth, dampening the very joy that I was chasing on my road to healing…

What if the enemy pulls the rug out from under me and I completely crumble?

What if when I face him again, my spirit breaks, and I find myself back in the same dark, heavy, and painful place?

And here's the real question…

What if embracing this new joy is really only setting me up to fall harder the next time?

What if chasing joy is really just placing a huge target on my back?

I mean, if I choose to live inside my comfort zone, the safe zone, and not stretch so far as to embrace an on-fire, light-shining, Jesus-loving, skirt-spinning joy, would that truly be better in the end? Because, let's face it… I can't go back there. I just can't.

And I'm willing to bet that as you are reading through those, some of you are facing the same joy-restricting thoughts (*and lies*). In chapter seventeen, we are going to deeply explore how to begin the process of taking back control of our thoughts to allow God's peace and rest to pour freely through our hearts. But for the purpose of this chapter, let's take a quick moment, a brief pause, and focus on another important element in our struggle with fear… The frequent instigator.

You see, the enemy hates our joy and even more, he hates the way that it reflects back to our One True Healer, Jesus. He would love nothing more than to keep us in this place, tormented by the what-ifs and the overwhelming fear of the unknowns. Why? Because when we face these doubts, these fears, these worry-filled spirals, he knows that we will oftentimes choose the familiar comfort of our play-it-safe patterns while he continues his warfare on our hearts and on our calling.

"Don't step out," he whispers. *"Don't be naïve. Can you really face that kind of gut-wrenching pain… again? Expect nothing, step into nothing, trust no one, and you'll be safe. That fullness and joy is just not realistic. It's not worth it. This is your compromise. This is your path to survival."*

Sound familiar? It's paralyzing. I promise I've been there. But I am looped back to a day when God stepped into that fear, into my own spiral, and taught me

122

something absolutely life-changing about seeking His glory when I'm feeling overwhelmed by my fears. Let's start here...

Faith, Fear, and His Glory

I have frequently heard the saying, *faith and fear cannot occupy the same space*, but while this is ideally true that if we genuinely have faith in God, believe in His love for us and rest in His plan for our lives, it will remove all fear from our hearts, it's just not fully attainable for me in most circumstances. And here's the thing, *I'm not interested in being fake with you.*

While I prefer the more grace-filled statement, *faith over fear*, I'll be the first to tell you that realistically, this is not always fully achievable for me either. *However,* it does allow space for growth and it communicates the more helpful message that my fears are not evidence of my failure as a believer, but often a normal human reaction to present life circumstances.

I believe that it's important to be real and transparent on this journey with you, so I wanted to share something very personal here. It's a peek into my own struggle, at times, to fully lean into faith over fear. Here's a personal journal entry that I wrote in the middle of my season of healing...

Ever feel like your circumstances do not look like His promises, or worse, His goodness? Like your storm is swirling and it is threatening to overtake you. You keep repeating the mantra, God is good, but inside you feel the panic begin to rise. The familiar internal struggle begins as the fear grows. Wait, I know God is good and I know He loves me. But, this storm... It's terrifying and I just feel so overwhelmed! You soon find yourself tossed about the boat, hit by waves of sadness, confusion, anxiety, fear, frustration, pain, and even anger.

If this is part of God's promise, it doesn't look like you expected it to look. It doesn't feel like you expected it to feel. And you're trying so hard to just hold on and keep the faith, but the undeniable truth is that you don't know what's coming next and you begin to fear its impact.

You strain your eyes to find Jesus through the sheets of rain in front of you, but your spirit is sinking deeper with each slam of your body against the rails.

You're just about ready to accept defeat and you think this situation can't possibly get much worse, but then the real doubt begins to set in...

Maybe the promises that you heard from your Heavenly Father have been reversed. Maybe He just didn't show up. You find yourself rationalizing it. Maybe I heard Him wrong? Or, maybe I fell short in doing my part. Maybe I just wasn't enough. I wasn't good enough. It's easy for me to accept that explanation because it's familiar. Always falling short. Always failing. And you find yourself releasing a cry from the deepest part of your soul. Jesus, please help me!

And in that moment, my friends, I felt completely overwhelmed and terrified. Again, *faith over fear* just wasn't always (and still isn't always) realistic for me.

But here's the best part... In those painful moments when I lost my trust, my confidence in Him, He faithfully reached in and scooped me up. He held me, loved me, reassured me, strengthened me, and redirected me. And let me share with you His powerful four-word life-changing lesson that began to shift everything...

Step. Into. Your. Authority.

You see, that day when I was eyeball deep in my worry-filled thoughts and fears and on the verge of tipping into total panic, painfully close to reverting back to the old habit of hiding myself away because it just felt safer, He gently stepped in and reminded me who He was and who I am in Him. And the first part of His lesson that day was all about glory...

"My child, which comes first... faith or glory?"

His question seemed simple. The answer, obvious... Faith, of course. If you focus on having faith over fear, especially through the storms, you'll be rewarded with glory, right?! But, as soon as the answer settled into my thoughts, something about it just didn't sit right. And I couldn't quite put my finger on it.

"What is glory?" I eventually asked Him, as I processed the word through my own life-experience filter...

Study for the grade. Achieve the A... Glory.

Practice every day. Make the winning shot... Glory.

Push endlessly to be the perfect spouse and perfect parent. Have the perfect family... Glory.

Work harder. Do more. Go beyond... Glory.

Have enough faith.... Glory.

And friends, I'm here to tell you that as much as I should know the difference between *religion* and *relationship* by now, sometimes when I'm struggling in a storm, I still manage to confuse the two. His nudge was a gentle reminder that day letting me know that I was straining and focusing on the wrong thing. And here's why...

Glory, by a worldly definition, is the ultimate destination, most often achieved by hard work and dedication to a specific desired result. It's the end-goal. It's the mark of success. It's the finish line. It's the gold medal. The Lombardi trophy. It's the big house and the big career.

Glory, by a religious definition, is the touch and favor of God in your life that you are able to earn through faith, dedication, and service. The harder you work, and the more faith you have, the more favor and love God gives to you. (Don't worry if this doesn't sit right with your spirit. It shouldn't.)

Glory, *by a relationship definition*, is both beautifully and simply the indescribable experience of sitting in the *very real* presence and love of God, a tangible and truly personal relationship, connection, and outpouring.

It's the Holy Spirit entering your space. It's an exposure to God, His works, His goodness, and His love that is undeniably life-changing. It's the moments when His voice, His touch, and His presence become a permanent footprint on your life because you realize that there is no love like His.

And hear this: It is *not* a result of something we work to earn or faith it until we make it. It is given. Freely. And it is the purest definition of love.

In reflecting on that last definition, I am reminded of so many experiences that I have had with my Heavenly Father over the last year. Moments when He flooded my vehicle with His presence, *just because*. Moments where His voice calmed every fear that filled my heart. Moments when He whispered, "Watch for my love notes today" and I was left in complete tears by the very tangible evidence of His heart.

In each and every one of those instances, fear, anxiety, doubt, confusion, and anger, all the what-ifs and the unknowns, they began to fall away. Why? Because when I was in His presence, I *knew* without a doubt that if I gave it all over, He would hold me, guide me, and carry me.

His presence *is* a blanket that wraps around your heart. Your spirit can not only sense, but deeply *feel* His very real and tangible promises...

You are safe. Rest in me. I love you.

Glory, *the experiencing of His presence and our very real relationship with Him*, is our pathway to peace in the storm. But that's not where the lesson ended...

Because conquering our fears is not just about leaning in, but also about stepping in, into our authority that is. He knew that there was another aspect of this issue that I needed to be reminded of and it was this...

When I am with you, the enemy has no choice but to flee. And he will. My child, walk confidently in that truth today.

You see, although the enemy would love to convince me that I am forever trapped in his lie-filled spiral of fear, the truth that I am reminded of once again is that he only has as much power as I give him. I know that I will inevitably face difficult days, painful circumstances, and rainy seasons, but *he will never have the power to make me crumble. He will never have the power to steal my joy.* I may crack. I may bend, even. But he cannot break me.

What a story-changing paradigm shift!

The truth is that I walk every day with the one true King and when the enemy tries to make me cower, I simply have to remind Him of my authority in Jesus and I can watch him as he flees! It's so important we remember that God's heart is for us and recognize this authority that we carry through Him. We don't have to acknowledge, justify, or water the enemy's lies until they root so deeply in our hearts that we find ourselves spiraling. We can demand he take his seeds back and burn them!

When the seventy-two disciples returned, they joyfully reported to him, "Lord, even the demons obey us when we use your name!"

"Yes," he told them, "I saw Satan fall from heaven like lightning! Look, I have given you authority over all the power of the enemy, and you can walk among snakes and scorpions and crush them. Nothing will injure you." (Luke 10:17-19 NLT)

Maybe you don't share the same fears that held me hostage, but other fears (or lies from the enemy) are dampening your joy. Today, I am inviting you to step into your authority in Jesus. Even though we may be tempted to cower in the enemy's presence because he tries to convince us that we are nothing, weak, and inferior, we must remember that, by the grace of God, we have the power to stand confidently in our authority and demand his retreat. We are not under the enemy's command...

We are daughters of the Most High King!

We are royalty.

Full Circle

So, let's bring this full circle. Here is the bottom line that God was guiding me to with His question about faith and glory ...

He is reminding us that if we rest in His glory and His presence, seek Him, spend time with Him, and delight in our moments with Him, then our fears of the unknowns and the what-ifs will be calmed by His steady reassurance that He's with us, He's for us, He loves us, and He's holding us.

Knowing Him, *truly knowing* Him, is once again the key. And get this...

As we seek to know Him and grow to fully and deeply understand His heart, as we personally experience His very tangible presence entering our space and His goodness pouring over our lives, the faith will begin to grow naturally from that relationship. It will wrap around our hearts, blanket our fears, and transform our spirit, giving us the strength and courage to step into our authority and demand that the enemy take back what is his.

Yes, my friends! We can do this!

That's a fear-conquering strategy that I can believe in and step into!

Our Father's presence *is* the paradigm shift.

You see, the truth is... I am *not* in some test-of-willpower cycle. I am *not* expected to force myself to *faith it into fruition*, only to find myself tripping over the same fear-filled rock or circumstance. I do *not* have to pretend that I am a strong warrior every day, in control and winning every battle over my fears. Where's the grace, or growth, in any of that? It's defeating.

And if you find yourself feeling defeated today, here is your reminder to pause. Let Him speak into your heart. And believe this...

The more we simply choose to delight in Him, invite Him into our day and grow to understand His heart, the more the trust and surrender will become a natural part of who we are.

So, which comes first... faith or glory?

Glory, my friends, always His glory.

He knows your storm. He knows the devastating mess that it has created in your heart. He knows you are doing your best and He knows your every fear. He is calling you to step into your authority over the enemy by *first* leaning into Him.

Rest and just *feel* Him. Let Him pour over you. *Your storm may not calm*, but you will find peace, renewed strength, courage, and reassurance in Him.

And when it all feels so overwhelming, and you find yourself in another painfully familiar worry-filled spiral or face-down in the dirt, I encourage you to remember this promise that He made to us…

I have told you these things so that you will be filled with my joy. Yes, your joy will overflow!

(John 15:11 NLT)

He's for you. And He loves you, unconditionally.

Chapter 13

Share the Journey

Friends, I know how tender your heart can feel, easily recoiled back into its safe space when you sense that you don't line up with what the world has said you should be. And I know that although life is full of humbling moments, the most painful ones usually involve a gross exposure of our cracks, flaws, and imperfections to the world.

I recently went through an experience that left me feeling wide open, exposed, and very vulnerable. I first fought the desire to crawl into a hole. Then, I fought the urge to act like everything was fine. Both options, either option, would have ultimately left me feeling empty. I knew that. But regardless of what I knew to be true deep down, it didn't change what I felt in that moment...

My heart desperately cried out for the hole, the safe place to hide, and my pride roared with need for the lie!

Why? Because when this kind of gross exposure happens, society tells us to immediately shift into damage control. The message is clear: *Hide your imperfections and cover up the pain with lies.*

Wear a smile. Act like nothing's wrong. Act like you're winning. Don't let anyone see your vulnerability. Don't let them see you crack. If they see it, it gives them power over you.

And when we listen to this advice of the world, we find ourselves so busy trying to avoid further damage and save face that we often feel a very real and terrifying internal struggle when we even consider another option, one that would allow someone into that very vulnerable place that we have grown to protect so well. And worse, we lose out on a huge opportunity to be uplifted and poured into by others during our own personal healing journey.

You see, I knew that there was another option, one outside of the choices of shame-induced hiding or pride-filled saving face. But I also knew that option C would not come easily for me because it brought with it even more vulnerability. The kind of vulnerability that paralyzed me with fear. The kind of fear that would shoot roots into the ground and effectively anchor me to whatever feeling or season that I was facing because I just couldn't bring myself to move forward.

"But God," I argued, *"if I let anyone in, they will witness the complete clutter and chaos behind my mask; the absolute disaster that I truly am."*

And the mere thought of that, and the rejection it would

inevitably bring, was more than my broken heart could bear.

But the truth is that nobody witnesses your clutter and chaos with such absolute clarity as Jesus. Nobody sees your messy, your shame, your insecurities, and your mistakes like He does. And I'll say it again, He can not only see the evidence of your imperfections, He can see your heart and all the things you try so hard to hide away. And yet, hear this...

He still runs to you, scoops you up in His arms, and says, "*My child, I love you. You are beautiful. You are mine. And I choose you.*"

And suddenly, we're reminded *(once again, as many times as it takes)* that we are loved, deeply and unconditionally. That when we begin to feel that familiar panic rise, the fear of judgement from those around us, we need only to take a moment, listen for His voice, and solidly re-anchor our identity in Him. Just Him. Just Jesus.

The truth is, anchoring my value to anything or anyone other than God exposes every part of my identity to the potential for soul-crushing cycles of instability and insecurity. I know this because I have had my own painful struggles with identity for a very long time, which we will beautifully explore more deeply in chapter fifteen. But here's the key that I want to touch on for the purpose of this chapter...

When we stand on the truth of who we are in God, no longer defined by the decisions, judgements, actions, or words of others, it suddenly gives us the courage and strength to allow real vulnerability to flow again. When we deeply secure and anchor ourselves in Him and then to allow that solid foundation of who *He says* we are to hold our hearts safe, it frees us to let down the veil of perfection, tear down the walls of protection, and beautifully extend and receive the life-giving and joy-giving messages of God's hope, healing, and love with each other.

And it's time, my friends, time to share the journey.

Share the beautiful. Share the hard. Share how He helped you. Share how He saved you. Share how He met you right where you were and wrapped His arms around you. Share your healing. Share your joy. Share your dancing. Just share.

While I pondered on this word, share, I was reminded of a time at my parent's farm recently. The grandkids were playing together by the campfire making big circles with some sparklers that we brought along for fun. As they began to troubleshoot how to most efficiently light them, I heard the oldest grandchild say to the younger ones, "Here, use mine to light yours!"

And it hit me...

Use mine to light yours.

Because when we share His blessings, we share His love and His heart, and it sparks something inside each other.

When we share our difficult, we open the door for others to love us through it, lift us up in prayer, and support us through the painful seasons of the journey, just as He intended.

And when we find our joy again, we are invited to share the story of how, by the grace and love of Jesus, we overcame.

We were never meant to carry any of it, and *especially* not all of it, alone.

Likewise, we were never meant to dance alone.

But there is a freeing, yet often difficult and terrifying, truth behind this idea and it is this…

We cannot truly minister to each other's hearts from behind the veil of perfection.

We cannot save face or hide our true selves away and simultaneously walk fully through His calling to lift and love on each other.

I don't know about you, but my heart has never allowed rest, vulnerability, and healing to flow with a friend that speaks from the pulpit of perfection. No, to the contrary, my heart has opened up and allowed life-giving hope to reach some of my deepest cracks and crevices from the friend that said, "I've been there. My life is not perfect. I often feel very broken. And I struggle too. Sometimes, I even fall flat on my face. But here is what God has been teaching me..."

And with that message, and God's nudge, the torch has been passed to me. I have the same power through Him to touch others; to share my journey, share my difficult seasons, and share how God healed me with His love and His grace. But it requires one vitally important (and sometimes scary and difficult) commitment from me:

I cannot fully embrace His calling on my heart unless I am willing to be imperfect.... Made perfect by His love.

Will others use the opportunity to mock, gossip, and hurt me? Of course... In fact, I have learned to expect it because the enemy loves to think that he can kill your spirit and the calling on your heart with the words, actions, and opinions of others.

But here's where he greatly underestimates me...

My identity is now strongly and securely anchored to God. And my heart is held completely safe in His steadfast and loving hands.

You see, the enemy doesn't stand a chance at breaking me when Jesus is the One that holds me. And the beautiful blessings and promises that come from walking in the path laid before me by my Heavenly Father will deem the enemy's attacks simply futile.

So, with a calling on our hearts and a commitment to the One who loves us so much that He holds us through the valleys, cries with us in the storms, and lifts us up to find peace and hope in His promises again, let's use our life to be His message.

Let's drop the protective veil of perfection and allow life-giving love, His love, to pour through our story as we share it with others.

Let's be a witness to His power as He uses us to bless and lift one another.

Use mine to light yours. And if you feel led, share back and light mine again. And if I share mine and you share yours, imagine the power of healing and joy that can reach beyond just you and me. Imagine what God can do with our messages and stories. Imagine what mountains He can move with our faith.

It doesn't have to be big. It doesn't have to be plastered on the walls for all to see. But today, I invite you to share.

Whatever season you are in, whatever blessings or hardships you face, find a heart you can trust and share what God is doing in your life.

Light each other. Lift each other.

The healing that you experience through sharing your story - the hope, peace, and joy that He pours into you as you rise and bring others with you - will absolutely be life-changing.

Chapter 14

The Painful Why's of Loss

I'm going to get a little real and raw with you today. It's often an uncomfortable topic, but I'm growing to understand that it has a purpose and a place in my processing and healing, and maybe yours too.

When God Shakes Things Up

Some of the most difficult parts of my journey have been when God reached in and shook things up unexpectedly. Dissolved friendships, dream job opportunities that ended, unanticipated closed doors, and painful boundaries that had to be drawn with people that I love. How could it be part of God's plan to remove things or people that I treasure and hold dear?

And, let's say that this is truly part of His plan, why then does it feel so extremely counterproductive to His message?

Shannon, I'm healing you. I'm walking you through this journey to the fulfillment of My promise. To the fulfillment of My joy. My vision for your future is more beautiful than you can imagine. But first, let Me just shift this relationship, move this career, dissolve this comfort, whatever it may be. Don't worry... I've got this... I promise. - God

I don't know about you, but each time this happens, I still struggle to understand. It often feels unfair and painful. It's confusing and I begin to question why. And yet every time I take it to Him, one thing is always made crystal clear...

"*I am in this*," is His gentle and unwavering reply.

So why does God sometimes remove things from our lives that leave a gaping hole in our heart or cause us discomfort? Brace yourselves...

I don't know.

The truth is that we are never promised an explanation. While it's true that there are times when His reasons are revealed later and those moments build our faith and reaffirm that His hands are always at work in our lives, there are often shifts and shakes that we may never understand. And that is when He calls us to trust Him the most.

Here is what we *are* promised... If we cling to Him and submit to His heart, even in our confusion or discomfort, even in our pain or loss, even in our anger, He will pour out His blessings in our lives and reweave those painful, dangling and tender loose ends into something indescribably beautiful for our hearts. Yes, it may hurt (*deeply*) for a while, but He is always working in the details and He is omniscient.

Our Heavenly Father can see infinitely beyond what is within the scope of our understanding. And even though we often don't understand a door that closes or a friendship that ends, He loves us too much to only operate within the restrictions of our reasoning. And the truth is, as much as I crave control when my world feels so increasingly chaotic, I don't want to rest my hope of the future in my own plans. I know, deep down, that joy is not found within the limited scope of what I can see and understand. Aligning myself with His vision and His plan - that is His desire for my heart - because there is no greater promise than the one we have in Him.

In other words, He is inviting us to step out in the faith and confidence that His design and His vision for our lives is far better than we could ever imagine.

But to be honest, sometimes I contemplate what it would be like if I could peek at the blueprints detailing what God has planned for me. I imagine how it would change the way that I process the current phase of construction that I'm in or the things that He's shifting and shaking up around me and within me. Having the opportunity to see such final details would surely remove any doubt, I reason. However, as much as I present this seemingly solid argument on my end, His response lovingly remains, "*I am in this. Trust me.*"

You see, we may not always understand, and it may not always feel fair, but we can rest and find peace if we trust that He is preparing us for something far greater. He is aligning us with His vision and the blessings that He has in store for our lives and our hearts. And that simple but beautiful truth, watered and allowed to take root, is where we anchor our hope when He shakes things up without explanation.

The Other Kind of Loss

But while it can be extremely uncomfortable and even painful when God reaches in and shakes things up in our lives like friendships and jobs, I cannot even begin to compare that kind of loss to the absolutely unimaginable loss of a child, a spouse, a loved one, a marriage, or the deep suffering and life-changing experience of illness or abuse.

There are some losses that carry extreme pain and can only be truly honored and closely understood by someone who has walked through that same difficult season. It's not to say that the loss we experience with God's shifting and shaking is somehow unimportant or trivial. No, all loss deserves to be acknowledged, poured through, felt, and healed. It's just to say that if you have walked through such tremendous pain as this, I'm not here to pretend that I know and fully understand the extreme suffering you have felt or the deep mourning and grief that you have experienced. And I want you to hear my heart right up front when I say that I'm not trying to pretend or present that I can, or that I do. I deeply honor your pain.

This kind of loss is just so difficult to process. We are already mourning the event, the person, the marriage, the season, or our own sense of identity, but then there is the excruciating piece of the puzzle that frequently sits painfully unanswered... Why, God? Why?

You see, I emotionally process and navigate change much better when I can dissect it, place reasoning into it, and begin to somewhat understand it. But the painful truth about this kind of loss is that there is often no easily identifiable or understandable explanation at all. And when this happens to myself or someone that I love, I still find myself asking God why He didn't intervene. Why sometimes...

The marriage doesn't mend.

The loved one doesn't get well.

The prognosis is terminal.

The house is foreclosed on.

The life is forever changed.

The moment is forever gone.

And the void left behind is forever deep.

And that's why this part of the chapter is so heavy. So very heavy. Because when this happens, my heart absolutely breaks. There is nothing that I can say to adequately describe or do justice to the brokenness that my loved one feels.

But can I share something with you that He has so often poured into me in those fragile and life-shattering moments?

He is there, always with us in that broken place, always holding us and comforting us, calling us nearer to Him so that He can pour His love over us.

And if you find yourself in that space, know that He is *weeping with you* and for you, right now, because He loves you so much. You are His beloved child and He hurts so deeply when you travel through seasons that leave you completely shattered.

This is not the end of your story, I promise. This book, this message of healing, hope, and joy, is meant for you too. Life may never look the same. It may have forever bent you. But He will help you through it. And He has a purpose for you, a calling on your heart, that will pour life back into you someday. For now, just seek rest in Him, feel His presence, and let Him hold you.

A few years ago, a friend posted something on her social media that I'll never forget and it just seems so fitting for this moment...

She wrote that it often made her upset when people would use the phrase, *God will never give you more than you can handle.* You see, my friend had lost her child, a pain that I truly cannot even begin to fathom. And while sometimes people are well-meaning in their support, they can be incredibly uncomfortable and awkward around unimaginable loss and grief. I am that person, friends.

If I might take a detour here for just a minute...

Sometimes I have really good and true intentions in my heart but in my awkward and jumbled attempt to provide comfort and support, I just don't come anywhere close to saying what I actually mean. In fact, I have found myself completely rambling my way through an uncomfortable expression of my feelings, telling a friend's father that his son, a former classmate of mine, was a beautiful person and I was so very sorry for his loss, only to end the conversation with, "I hope you have a beautiful Christmas." No joke. *That* came out of my mouth. And then I cried... for hours... because I couldn't believe that in a moment of awkward and anxiety-filled *how do I end* panic, I had said something so insensitive and likely so painful to this already-grieving father. So, I say all that to say this... If you're in this kind of extremely difficult and painful season, please give us awkward ones a little grace and benefit of the doubt. We are trying, I promise.

But, looping back to my friend's response to the often-painful phrase that *God will never give us more than we can handle*, she quite gracefully navigated the situation, turning it into a powerful reminder about our Heavenly Father, and I will truly never forget how her message hit my heart that day. Here is what she so beautifully reminded us all...

It is in *those* moments when it *does* become more than we can handle that we are reminded to bring it to Him and lay it at His feet. To just fall into His arms, His grieving and broken-hearted baby girl curled up on her Heavenly Father's lap, and let Him hold us and carry us through the rest.

You see, we will *absolutely* face more than we can handle in this life, but that's when we draw the closest to His heart and seek His healing touch. Because friends, when our world shatters into a million pieces and the weight of it all threatens to leave us forever broken, forever destroyed, He promises that we will never be left to carry it or piece it back together alone.

Loss and Joy

So, let's bring this full circle. Let's explore the idea of grabbing joy and pulling it into even the most painful seasons. What would that look like? Can the two even exist in the same space?

First, let's clear some clutter so that we can truly hear His Heart as we explore those questions...

He is *not* asking us to fake the day with words of joy, hope, and peace while our hearts are feeling anything but. To be honest, that not only creates another burden on our already bruised and broken spirits, but it is also the perfect recipe for resentment and brokenness in our relationship with Him. No, that's definitely not the space that He's gently calling us into for healing *and* joy.

147

Your Heavenly Father knows your heart and He loves you immensely and unconditionally. He understands that when you face a season of earth-shattering loss, or even the purposeful but painful shifting and shaking orchestrated by His loving hands, you may find your hope rattled. Deeply rattled. Yes, He knows that an extremely painful season may rock your faith and uproot your joy. He has seen how it causes you to question the goodness of His promises or the very existence of His presence in the hard.

And can we be honest for a moment? It *has* shaken mine before… greatly. But here's God's truth that broke through the pain, the anger, and the doubt…

When my heart is deeply suffering and I begin to question it all (*even His goodness*), my incredible Heavenly Father always gently and lovingly wraps His arms around me and reminds me that it's okay to bring it all to Him. Yes, *all* of it.

You see, shame-filled messages that expect us to never doubt God's decisions or be shaken by them ignore the truly beautiful, game-changing factor and gift that He freely gave us on the cross, His grace.

The truth is, I believe that there is no shame in our admission of fear, doubt, or anger. God already knows it's there. He knows your heart and His desire is that you bring the authentic you to His table; to draw close to Him as He guides you, holds you, and heals you. He wants your whole heart, unreserved and fully open.

He doesn't fault you or condemn you for having fears and doubts. He simply wants you to bring those fears and those doubts *to Him*.

Remember, you don't have to clean up *anything* before you come to Him. You don't have to clean up the confusion, the pain, or the shame. He loves you and He is asking you to invite Him in; into your heart, into your pain, into your confusion, and into your healing. He will walk with you through the hard, and even if you are angry *with Him*, He will always hold you.

We are going to face things on this journey that leave us beaten and bruised. We are going to face circumstances prayerfully believing that He will give us the mind-blowing, earth-shattering miracle that we want. And sometimes, the mountain will remain unmoved. We will find ourselves confused, grieved, and even angry. But in those moments when we find ourselves struggling the most to lean into Him, if we pause, we can hear Him gently reminding us...

I know you don't fully understand or see me in this. I hear the desperate cries of your heart. But I promise, my child, I am taking these broken pieces and I will pour my healing into them. My heart is always for you.

And while we don't always understand His plans and we can't always reason our way through how such unimaginable losses happen in our lives or why, He's asking us to lean in and trust Him with our future. Trust that He loves us. Trust that He has our heart at the forefront of His mind, always. Trust that He will faithfully see us through this deep pain and wilderness and we will be standing on different ground tomorrow, even if the answer or the path is not the one we so desperately sought.

It does not mean that it's always easy.

It means that, like my friend so beautifully reminded us, we always know Who we can turn to when it's not.

So, whatever you are facing today, whether it's because you have suffered an unimaginable loss or God is reaching in and shaking things up in your world today, removing, moving, closing, and shifting, be sure of one thing…

He loves you and He is there. You are seen. You are known. And you are deeply loved.

Reflect and remember the moments that He has stepped in and worked miracles in your life. Remember how His presence and His voice has seen you through difficult times in the past. And, when you find yourself in the fetal position on the floor, struggling to see a future that offers anything resembling hope or joy, bring yourself back to this:

"I have cared for you since you were born. Yes, I carried you before you were born. I will be your God throughout your lifetime - until your hair is white with age. I made you, and I will care for you. I will carry you along and save you." (Isaiah 46:3-4 NLT)

And I'd like to share one more verse with your heart today…

But even if we are faithless, he will still be full of faith, for he never wavers in his faithfulness to us! (2 Timothy 2:13 TPT)

He is always faithful, even if we momentarily lose faith in Him, because He is a good and loving Father, and He is inviting us to anchor our hearts to that truth today.

Chapter 15

Redefining Perfection

Let's take a minute and talk about the elephant in the room… Imperfection. We work so hard to be the perfect wife, perfect mom, perfect daughter, perfect sibling, employee, friend, boss, Christian, neighbor, woman… whew! I'm exhausted just writing it.

But, let's face it… Trying to chase perfection is like trying to put a fitted sheet on our king-size bed. You see, we recently added this 4" foam mattress topper that makes the bed extra comfy, but it also creates a real struggle when attempting to get the fitted sheet secured in place. You get the final corner nice and snug and you feel so proud, and then another corner just pops right off. So, you move around, re-tuck that corner down and get it looking neat and perfect and well… up pops the next one. It's a never-ending round and round as you struggle to get it looking flawless. And one day as I found myself fighting our sheets, willing them to stay in place for more than a few minutes, I began to realize…

Sometimes, I get the mom thing right, then the spouse thing goes wrong. Sometimes, I get the friend thing perfect and am feeling really good and then the daughter thing goes awry. Sometimes the work or homeschool day goes really well and then I bomb at being loving and patient with my family at night. Sound familiar? I quickly find myself on this hamster wheel, chasing perfection in everything I do. I'm absolutely exhausted and feeling like a failure at every turn. And yet, no matter how endless and unrewarding this pursuit feels, each morning I wake up and it begins again.

Ahhh... yes, the hamster wheel of perfection.

I won't lie to you... Even in the never-ending process of defeat and exhaustion, there was a time in my recent past when I found the chase much more comfortable and far more tolerable than the thought of my only other alternative...

Letting go and letting people (and God) accept and love me for who I am, including loving myself.

You see, I could go into all the details of why I chase perfection, but as I have peeled the onion layers back little by little, I've ultimately determined that the root cause comes down to one simple but frustrating lie – *I'm just not enough.* And over time, I've realized that the fear and anxiety associated with that lie are what drives me to climb back on that hamster wheel of defeat every single day.

The truth is, when I take time to more deeply reflect on this pattern, I begin to recognize that each time I climbed on the hamster wheel, I would run harder, faster, and longer only to find myself in the same spot as when I started. Even worse, despite all of my running, all of my efforts to be more, do more, and accomplish more, I never met the end of a single day with feelings of peace or confidence... I wish! Instead, each night as I placed my head on the pillow, I would silently resolve that when I woke up the next morning, I would chase "being more" ... again. But next time, I'll do it *better*.

Where did we get this idea that "being more" is the only thing that will make us worthy and bring us fulfillment? And why did I have this sneaking suspicion that it was robbing me of all the joy that Jesus had in store for me?

Because it did, my friends. And it does. The truth is, chasing perfection robs us of the joy of our present and the peace of knowing that we are perfectly and wholly loved today, just as we are, by the One who loves us the most!

And let me hit the pause button right here, because if you are like me, a recovering perfectionist and people-pleaser, I may have just hit another tender spot for you... The need to be the "perfect Christian" in order to make Jesus proud. You see, sometimes we even find ourselves on the hamster wheel in our spiritual walk:

I'm not doing enough or being enough for God. I need to read more, pray more, go to church more, or be more like Jesus. I am not a perfect follower, not even close, and He's probably so ashamed of me; so disappointed that I haven't worked harder to live up to His calling and His expectations. Look at all these people around me doing so much better at this.

Another failure. Another defeat.

Another lie.

And it steals our joy, our peace, our hope... and our calling.

Don't ever forget that there is a powerful promise and truth that will always exist *between* God's love and calling on our hearts and the enemy's taunting and defeating perfection-chasing lies: *the Cross.*

Where the former recognizes that we are made imperfectly perfect in Him, loved and enough, forgiven and covered in grace, the latter denies every important truth and promise made to us that day when Jesus traded His life for ours.

You are loved, wholly and unconditionally... Yesterday. Today. Tomorrow. And always. And you will *always* be more than enough.

His grace and His love – We don't have to earn it. We don't have to try harder, do more, or be more. Once again, we are called to simply draw close to Him and allow the rest to become an extension of a life beautifully intertwined with His.

Friends, hear this... *We are not compared against each other for daily worthiness of His outpouring, standing in line to receive our portioned amounts of love and grace as determined by the works we have achieved.*

No. It's simply and beautifully a gift. Freely given each and every day, in equal measure. Believe this and let it truly take root... He loves you, imperfections and all. And He loves you today, just as you are.

While it's absolutely true that we are called to "*live a life filled with love, following the example of Christ*" (Ephesians 5:2 NLT), and to seek ways to share His love with others, we are *not* expected to be perfect.

We are expected to anchor our hearts, our peace, and our hope to His love and allow His truths to define us. We are expected to rest in His love and grace and meet each day seeking His heart, letting Him love on us, and then *allowing some of our overflowing cup to beautifully leak out and pour onto others*.

It's not an expectation of *doing* or *being* more... It's a natural process and by-product of simply inviting Him in and sharing our life with Him.

Do you feel some weight lifting yet? I really pray that you do.

Stepping off the Hamster Wheel

So how do we take that first step? How do we trade our running shoes for dancing shoes? How do we give up this defeating and soul-crushing cycle and find joy in the letting go?

Speaking from my own journey, if we want to truly begin to break the cycle of chasing perfection, the process starts with taking a good look at what is really driving us. It's asking one very important question: What is at the core of this pursuit?

And when I took a deep look at my own hamster wheel last year, I found some interesting connections that helped me start processing and changing some of my perspectives. I wanted to share them here because I have a sneaking suspicion that some of you may find these relatable as you read through them:

I was always comparing myself to others around me, consistently watering thoughts of inadequacies in every area. No matter what it was, someone I knew did it better, and I never felt that my efforts (or my talents) were enough.

I walked away from every conversation with the replay on repeat, analyzing *everything* that I had said and how it may or may not have been pleasing to others. I wondered endlessly how they felt about me, what they thought of me, and if I became a topic of negative conversation once I left.

I felt anxious about allowing people to get close to me because I knew that if I allowed someone into my highly protected inner space, then they may find all my "muchness" to be just too much.

If I did something, especially for someone else, I had to do it perfectly or else I fell short and felt anything but proud. There was no gray area for me. Either I did it fantastic and without error, mind-blowing and a huge success, or I had failed.

I justified and defended my feelings and/or opinions at every turn, not because I felt the need to be right, but because I felt that if someone agreed with me, then it would reassure my heart that everyone in the room didn't think me stupid or unworthy to sit at their table.

I was the "yes" girl. At work, with friends, with family. I committed myself to every project, committee, task, and need. And when I committed, it had to be at a 200% or I left feeling that I had let someone down. I worked hours into the night and on weekends, sacrificing endlessly "for others." But I grumbled endlessly too.

I convinced myself daily that my family got the short end of the stick when they got saddled with me. That another mom probably plays Nerf wars more and has more patience. That another wife probably cooks more and listens better. That I am failing daily to simply... *be more*... for my own family. And I carried the weight of that guilt the most. To ease some of the shame, I resolved that I would do little or nothing for myself because I was already failing to do enough for them.

And I was tired. I was so very tired. Tired of working hard to keep my messiness under wraps. Tired of acting quiet and reserved to prevent the rejection of my muchness. Tired of feeling unsafe around others and churning with anxiety. Tired of feeling like I never live up to anything, look right, perform well, or say the right things. And not just tired. Realistically, that's an understatement. I was utterly and completely defeated and exhausted. And eventually I reached a point where it was easier to just exclude *all* the people and *all* the things than it was to hold up the act any longer.

Loneliness became a preferred option to the inevitable rejection that would crush my heart with the next blow.

Now let's refocus for a moment, take a big deep breath, and dive a bit deeper into some of the underlying themes here... A desire to be accepted, worthy, important, significant, special, and loved. The fear and insecurity (*ugh, I personally cringe at that word*) that I will be abandoned, hurt, or rejected. And the deeply rooted belief that I have to work really hard to be perfect so that I could achieve one in order to avoid the heart-shattering pain of the other.

But there was one very important truth that all of this (*all of it*) was missing and, when I found myself utterly exhausted from the never-ending hamster wheel and desperately ready to trade in my running shoes, God gently and lovingly stepped in and reminded me...

"My child, your identity is in Me. Only Me. I love you. I will never leave you or abandon you."

Because that's truly what it all comes down to, right? Our identity. And for as long as I can remember, my identity was like a piece of putty that I walked around placing in other people's hands, allowing them to mold me and shape me, to define me and determine my worth, while I nervously waited to see what they handed back and I painfully fretted over if they would decide that I was *enough*. There's that word again... *enough.*

But in that moment, I realized that God was calling me to recognize the brokenness of my patterns, the untruths that came with my ways of determining and defining my value, to finally let go of my desperate chase of perfection and to give my defeating cycle over to Him, fully.

He was calling me to allow Him to work through it; to let Him pour through me and speak life into my heart; *to allow His truths to become so deeply rooted in my spirit that they grow to become the beginning and the end of my identity*, reassuring my heart that I will never be abandoned or alone and I'm always more than *enough.*

An identity that is no longer putty, freely given to anyone and everyone. No, an identity that is securely anchored by solid truths tethering my heart to His.

So, if you find yourself relating to this chapter, if you find yourself struggling with your own hamster wheel of perfection, I urge you to remember this...

Your identity rests in Him, alone! Nobody else and nothing else determines your value, dictates your worth, or defines your beauty.

Nobody else gets to decide if you are loveable, worthy, or enough. And once you've fully allowed Him to reassure your heart of that truth, hear this…

You are chosen.
1 Thessalonians 1:4

You are loved.
Romans 5:8

You are the cherished daughter of the King.
You are royalty.
1 John 3:1-2

You belong here.
Jeremiah 1:5

You are beautifully made just as you are.
Psalm 139:13-16

You have special gifts that only you bring to the world.
You are irreplaceable.
1 Peter 4:10

You have a purpose.
Ephesians 2:10

You have a light.
Matthew 5:14

You are special.
Jeremiah 31:3

An identity that is no longer putty, freely given to anyone and everyone. No, my friends, an identity that is securely anchored by solid truths tethering your heart to His.

You are known.
Psalm 139:17-18

...

You are far more than *enough*.

Your family is blessed to have you.

Your friends are blessed to have you.

We are blessed to have you.

And it's your time to bloom!

Are you ready? I'm ready! But there's one more thing we need to remember and it is this...

Joy does not come passively. We must commit to it, push towards it, and grow. And in that growth, we will beautifully bloom! Let me explain...

Joy Does Not Come Passively

The truth is, changing old patterns, especially deeply rooted thought patterns, doesn't happen overnight. In order to really achieve the full freedom of knowing our identity in Him and fully resting in it, we will have to seek and embrace *change* in our thoughts, beliefs, and habits.

Make no mistake, giving up on the hamster wheel of chasing perfection can be challenging. Basically, it's a complete shift in perspective and a complete re-alignment of where we anchor ourselves. And simply put, such change often takes time.

163

It takes planting, watering, and committing to re-plant when His truths get uprooted, again. It takes speaking life into His words, even if we don't *feel* them in our hearts just yet. It's the action of taking His truths and declaring them over our lives and taking steps each day to *hold onto them* and lean into them.

In reality, as a recovering people pleaser, I have chased perfection my whole life, trying to be worthy of everyone's love and acceptance, running harder with each passing day. So for me, trading in my running shoes for dancing shoes was, and still is, a process. I continually have to sift through my feelings and my thoughts and realign them with what I know to be His truths.

But, there's one big (life-changing) difference in my processing and realigning now... Instead of chasing the idea of perfection defined as the pursuit of "being more," I redefined perfection as simply drawing ever closer to Him and embracing what He says about me today, right now, just as I am. Nothing extra. Nothing more. Simple, natural, and just as He made me; just as He sees me.

The beautiful and freeing truth is this... Jesus doesn't make mistakes and you are the daughter of a King.

If you are always trying to be something else, how can you share the unique and amazing gifts that He gave you?

If you hide in the shadows because you fear rejection, how can you shine for His glory in just the way He designed you to shine?

He made you. Every intricate detail. He chose you. He breathed life into you. He loves you. He accepts you. And it's time. He is calling you to replace your running shoes with dancing shoes and find joy again! But in order to do that, we must first be willing to do this...

We have to change our focus from chasing perfection to simply chasing His heart instead.

He has a calling on your life. He has a purpose for you. You are "*you*" for a reason. He desires a relationship with you and wants to give you His heart. So, when we stop chasing worldly acceptance, fleeting, temporary, and fickle, we will find joy and peace beyond understanding in His love and acceptance.

We will find a relationship with Jesus that will heal all the holes in our hearts that we have been trying to fill with everything else.

So, I just want to encourage you today...

Evaluate what you are chasing. Redefine perfection. You do not need to be more. You shine brilliantly just as you are. If you are not invited to someone else's table, don't hide in shame. Don't allow your identity to be like putty placed in other's hands for their molding and shaping. *There is always a place for you at His table.* Don't let fear of the world's rejection render you immobile. Anchor to Him. Shine bright for Him. And seek daily to truly know Him. For it is in chasing His heart, not in chasing perfection, that you will find rest, peace, and unending joy.

Chapter 16

The Brokenness Around You

As we journey through this chapter, I think you'll find that in some ways, it is a continuation of the message in the previous chapter. But you see, I believe that there is one more topic, a deeper and possibly more challenging factor, that is so important to our processing and healing. So, bear with me for a few seconds as we review a couple of connecting points in chapter fifteen before we truly dive into what I mean...

Remember the part where we discussed that allowing my worth or value to be defined by the words or actions of others can be one of my biggest barriers to finding joy? The putty concept, right? And remember how we focused on taking steps to realign and deeply anchor our identity to His truths instead of the broken world around us? So incredibly powerful and life-changing.

Except that sometimes this idea feels oversimplified.

Sometimes it can be quite challenging when someone we love is traveling through a difficult season as well. Sometimes, we realistically need a few *extra* tools. And that's why this chapter was so important to share.

Because you see, when we are on this journey chasing peace and joy and *someone we love* is also struggling with brokenness, it is often much harder to anchor ourselves, to find that solid ground. Sometimes their words or actions can be carved so deeply into our hearts that it flips our identity inside out in a matter of minutes. Sometimes we don't know how to truly protect our hearts around the people that are already allowed into our most vulnerable spaces. And if you find yourself in that place right now, I want to reassure you that...

You are not alone, you are seen, and God will be faithful. He will pour into you to help you through this pain and confusion. Keep your eyes on Him and keep your heart tender to *His touch*.

We are all human and, as such, we are all imperfect and broken, made perfect by our faithful and loving Heavenly Father. We know that pain finds us all at some point in this life. We may suffer betrayal, deep loss, rejection, hurt, or worse. And the truth is, residual scarring from a difficult season may lead some of us to be hurtful with our words or actions.

Now, let's assume for a moment that someone who has traveled, or is traveling through, a difficult season is directing such hurtful words or actions towards us. If that person is a stranger, it is a bit easier to anchor ourselves to what Jesus says about us and not let their actions truly penetrate our hearts. After all, how can someone define you who doesn't truly know you?

But what if it is someone we love and trust? What if it is someone that truly knows us, deeply, and we find some truths in their painful words? What can we do if we are on this journey chasing joy and someone we love is in a darker, painful place and their words or actions are truly hurting us and keeping us in a painful cycle of insecurity?

I'm stopping here for a moment to make an important distinction and clarification: When we speak of hurtful words or actions in this chapter, it is assuming a situation that is not abusive. We do not encourage anyone to accept or remain in any sort of abusive situation. Please seek help immediately if you are being abused.

As we know, pain can often lead to an entire host of other emotions, such as resentment, jealousy, and anger. When treated, there can be a path to healing. But sometimes, those feelings take up space in one's heart and instead of healing, they may temporarily burrow deeper into a darker place. The saying goes that hurt people hurt people. So, when we pause for a moment to recognize the pain that they must be carrying and pray for them, we can find rest in the faith that we serve a God who can move mountains. He is often working in the unseen and He *will* help us extend grace beyond even our own understanding.

Although I know that it is definitely not the easiest in these very difficult times, taking authority over our own response and allowing ourselves the emotional space to pause, breathe, and reflect on our own journey, recognizing that most of the time the other individual is likely also in deep pain, has the power to dramatically change the way that we view the situation. Shifting our focus to this perspective often allows us to empathize with them and take a moment to pray for them. Now, let me take a quick break to clarify what I mean...

This is not the...

Bless your heart, I'm praying for you because you desperately need a coming-to-Jesus moment, honey!

...kind of praying for them.

(You know what I mean, friends!)

This is the...

I truly care that you are suffering and I genuinely care about your heart!

...kind of praying.

And we don't need to make an announcement about it. We don't even need to tell them we are lifting their broken hearts daily. We just do it, silently and faithfully, because we love them and truly care about them. We want them to find peace and joy. We hurt for them because we know *firsthand* what broken feels like. We know *our own journey has needed grace, many times over, and we choose to pour it out onto them,* as well. And most importantly, we know we serve an incredible Father that loves them, immensely and unconditionally.

But there is also another significant and *very important* benefit to recognizing their pain, and it is this:

It allows us to see their words and actions for what they really are... Symptoms of brokenness, not truths that have the power to define us or shake us.

That is why there is a second prayer that I choose to lift up in moments like these. I ask Jesus to also protect my heart. I do not want to allow their words and/or actions to penetrate and define me. And that can be so incredibly difficult. So, I ask Him to help me discern the truth behind the words and remind me who I am in Him. It's a process and I'm still learning, but He's teaching me so much along the way.

The beautiful truth is that Jesus loves us all the same. We are *all* imperfect beings, broken in our own ways, and we are *not* loved more or deemed better by our Heavenly Father because of our stage in healing. He is working in *all* of our hearts. But, when it gets really hard to see through the pain of others, we must pull ourselves back to His truths again...

Only He has the authority to define who you are (and who they are) and He loves both of you more than you can imagine.

So, when we learn to pause and recognize the hurt in others, we can lift them up and simultaneously ask Jesus to continually remind us the truth of who we are in Him, and Him alone.

I am, once again, looped back to Proverbs 4:23, which says, "*So above all, guard the affections of your heart, for they affect all that you are. Pay attention to the welfare of your innermost being, for from there flows the wellspring of life.*" TPT

Everyone I know is hurting right now. The world has changed so much in such a short period of time and we are all trying to navigate through this new norm together. The future holds so many uncertainties and, in so many ways, we have no control over tomorrow. It's unfamiliar, stressful, exhausting, and sometimes frightening.

And during such a difficult time, it's especially important to be mindful of the seeds that we choose to plant and water in our hearts. Always remember this:

Don't let the enemy use a difficult season, or the words or actions of others, as an opportunity to deter you from where God is taking you. See the pain and symptoms of brokenness for what they are and lift it all up to Jesus.

On that note, I wanted to share with you a painful, yet big, lesson that God taught me about ten years back during our infertility journey. This story is neither my most beautiful moment, nor my most regretful, but it is one that I can bring myself to share:

To give you some background, leading up to the day of the incident, my husband and I had experienced several failed fertility treatment cycles and a recent miscarriage. We were midway through our second IVF cycle and because we lived in a very rural area, I was driving six hours roundtrip, three days per week, for fertility treatments. I was a ball of anxiety, stress, depression, and anger. On top of that, I was absolutely exhausted, physically and emotionally, and we were drowning in debt trying to have a family.

During my appointment that day, the doctor noted that he was discouraged by the progress of this new cycle and I left the appointment in a complete fog of pain, fear, and hopelessness. I headed to a store to pick up a few things before my long journey home. To this day, I cannot tell you what store I visited or what I had planned to pick up, but I can tell you with crystal clear clarity what happened next...

As I began to back out of my parking space, a car full of young men came flying around the corner and I quickly hit my brakes to avoid hitting them. They whipped into the spot next to me and the young man on the passenger side, probably in his early twenties, threw his door open while laughing and talking loudly. They were just kids having fun, but his door came within about an inch of hitting my car. And that was it. That's all it took. I completely lost it.

I yelled. I cursed. I threw my hands. I don't think the poor kid got a single word in. I honestly have no clue if he was attempting to apologize because in my anger-filled rant, I never even took a breath to notice.

I cannot imagine what I must have looked like in that parking lot, screaming at kids much younger than me and slamming my door. It makes me cringe just writing it. But then, when I was fully satisfied with my display of utter chaos and rage, as if I hadn't done enough, I squealed my tires out of that spot and well… I cried all the way home.

I was mortified, sad, embarrassed, and ashamed. Even as I write this, I want to hit the delete button so badly. It's difficult to admit how I allowed myself to react that way over something so trivial. It's difficult to admit that I was so clouded by anger, depression, fear, and exhaustion, that I didn't even recognize myself at that moment.

There have been many days that I have longed for the opportunity to go back and apologize to that young man. Although my actions were inexcusable, I wish I could explain. You see…

That person wasn't me. That person was hurting and scared and so very tired. That person was screaming in desperation and hopelessness; screaming that she simply didn't know how to carry all of it any longer; screaming that she needed someone to catch her and hold her; desperately wishing that someone would reassure her broken heart that everything was going to be okay.

But that poor young man didn't stand a chance to see, or know, any of that. All he witnessed that day was my utter and complete humiliating display of rage. How could he possibly know there was so much underlying pain? How could he know that this woman was truly screaming from some indescribably broken place deep within her and she didn't mean to hurt anyone, including him?

And how many times have we had someone in our lives like that? How many times have we known and loved someone that was traveling a painfully difficult season, deeply broken and hurting, and their words or actions have, in turn, caused us wounds? And not just any wounds, but deep, painful wounds that challenge our peace and our healing. Damage that begins to grow anger within us as well. A seeping infection that, if watered, begins to spread and causes more destruction around us.

So often all we see is the evidence of their brokenness, and all we feel is deeply attacked. It's truly difficult to see beyond the symptoms when we feel very hurt, especially when it's someone we love or care about. I have been on both sides of this situation and I know the struggle it presents to your heart.

You see, when someone I love is traveling through a difficult and dark season of brokenness and their words and actions penetrate that prayerfully placed armor, it often carves a much, much deeper wound. Why? Because such words and actions from someone I love and trust can place me painfully navigating through a disgusting mucky mess to determine what is true and what is not. And that is just plain hard.

So, how do we find joy today if the brokenness around us is attacking our peace and delaying our healing?

The truth is, when people we love hurt deeply, their hurt is often like a virus, a disease that attacks the heart and then quickly spreads to the people that they love most. And when something like that happens to us, it's so easy to feel justified in anger, frustration, harsh words, and bitter tones in return. Not only do we feel that our journey, our peace, and our healing have been compromised, but we feel deeply misunderstood and worse, completely unsupported.

And the difficult truth is, maybe in their brokenness, maybe in their pain, maybe they really can't, or don't, support and understand you. But also remember this…

When we feel like we are already hanging by a thread, that's exactly when the enemy attacks our thoughts, our words, and our hearts the most.

Hear this, my friends…

If you have someone in your life traveling through a season of brokenness, I'm not here to argue that you aren't justified in whatever emotions you feel today, but I am here to encourage you…

Do not allow the enemy to use the brokenness around you to steal away who you are becoming and what God is doing within you.

Take a few moments in this difficult season to focus on who you are in God and remember to pray tirelessly over your journey. Be diligent in lifting your heart, your thoughts, and your words to Him in prayer. Put on the armor of God and claim victory over an enemy that seeks only to destroy you *and* to destroy those you love.

Recognize that the brokenness around you most often comes from a place of deep pain and lay it at your Father's feet. Ask God to help you see their heart, and their journey, in a new light. Ask Him to pour over them with a love, peace, and rest that only He can provide.

The truth is, sometimes the brokenness around us will attempt to define and label us, robbing us on this journey, just as sometimes the brokenness within us will do the same to another. The enemy *always* has a plan littered with ways to keep us from ever reaching our joy and our calling. He will do whatever it takes to destroy you, your family, and the people you love most.

Pause and ask God to give you clarity and discernment in these difficult moments.

Reflect on the grace that you have so often needed and remember that God can help you extend that same grace to others.

Do not allow the enemy to use the brokenness around you to steal away who you are becoming and what God is doing within you.

God is leading us through the process of clearing our space, our hearts, to be able to fully receive what He's sharing and pouring out today. If it doesn't belong, *label it as such and give it to Jesus.*

He can help you heal. He will light the way. And if it's hurting someone you love, pause and pray for them. Because believe this, Jesus loves them too, so much!

There's no storm He can't handle and no mountain too big for Him to move today! We must simply and beautifully give it to Him and rest in His promise to work within it, within them, and within us.

Chapter 17

The Head Bone is Connected to the Heart Bone

Fill your thoughts with my words until they penetrate deep into your spirit. Then, as you unwrap my words, they will impart true life and radiant health into the very core of your being."
(Proverbs 4:21-22 TPT)

Two summers ago, a friend and I climbed Handies Peak in the beautiful San Juan Mountains of Colorado. It was my first fourteener and neither one of us trained (please don't follow my terrible example). The word *intense* might be an understatement, but I'll never forget how proud I was as we climbed our way up the mountain. We snapped photos and chatted with other hikers. We even laughed about our inability to breathe enough to laugh. It was a very lighthearted and fun morning. That is, until we rounded a corner and laid eyes on the last ascent. Once I saw that switchback-filled final stretch, my entire perspective changed and a feeling of heaviness poured over me. Instead of delighting in how far we had come, I quickly felt overwhelmed by what lay ahead and my heart sank. I suddenly grew very, very tired and each step became increasingly harder than the last, not just because of the altitude and difficult incline, but also because of one painfully important and telling shift...

My brain was now firing off doubt and my heart was starting to listen.

Thoughts are a powerful thing, aren't they? We can stand midway up the mountain and delight in how far we have come or we can stand midway up the mountain and feel completely overwhelmed by how far we still have to go.

Friends, we can look back at the ground we have covered on our journey to healing and joy, how far He has brought us, and feel absolutely uplifted and excited at the changes that we feel pouring through our hearts. Or, we can feel weighed down, overwhelmed, and even defeated by the residue and remnants that He is still working through in our healing today.

And how quickly my entire outlook changes when I switch my *thoughts,* my focus, from delighting in how far He has taken me to completely drowning in hopelessness over how far I still have to go. Why? I'll say it again... *Because when my brain starts firing off doubt, my heart begins to listen.*

Two things that God has been working to connect for me over the past year: My Head Bone and My Heart Bone. Changing old patterns. Controlling what thoughts I allow to take up residence. Because if they take up space in my mind, if I give them attention and water them, then I know this to be powerfully true...

They will absolutely take root in my heart and they *will* bear fruit, be it good or bad.

You see, as we will greatly explore in this chapter, *my thoughts* have the power to allow His life-giving messages and full outpouring of joy, peace, hope, and rest to freely flow into my heart OR they can completely bind it up, filter it, and restrict it from ever deeply rooting in my spirit at all.

And that is why He has encouraged me to continually dive deeper into this connection in my own life over the last year. Because guarding my thoughts equals guarding my heart. Because changing my thought patterns allows the fullness of His outpouring to reach deep into my spirit and His healing to follow.

As Proverbs 4:23 reveals, the feelings and thoughts that I decide to water and allow to take root (the place where I *choose* to anchor my heart), will undoubtedly affect not just a little of me, but *all* that I am.

So friends, if we're standing midway up our mountain and our knees are beginning to shake, here is our chance, our invitation, to pause and evaluate what thoughts we are letting in and what thoughts we are choosing to filter out. Where are we choosing to anchor our trust and our hope? What seeds are *you* choosing to water today?

You see, He is calling us to look back over our journey and be encouraged by the truth. Fear, shame, anger, anxiety, resentment, and unforgiveness are slowly washing off of us. He is walking us through radical healing. You, yes you, are *not* the same person that started this journey. And although there are still remnants that He is working through in your heart, in your story, you have already overcome so much!

Chasing joy, chasing healing, is a challenging, but beautiful journey and I've come to realize one really important thing in those moments when I feel overwhelmed: *Sometimes we have to look in the rearview mirror to truly appreciate how far He has brought us and allow that truth to encourage our hearts and bring us hope when we are facing a switchback-filled journey ahead.* So, let's explore that idea a bit more...

The Rearview Mirror

We often hear the phrase "in the rearview mirror" as a way to suggest that "it's in the past," and usually in the context of implying that we should leave something behind or let it go. But today, I want us to look in the rearview mirror, possibly even at some painful times in our lives, or at the beginning of this journey, as a way to find strength and courage for our next step forward. We are not trying to resurface the pain, but we are searching for God in the details and trust me, *He was there.*

Holding us.

Protecting us.

Carrying us.

Guiding us.

For just a moment, I'm asking you to pause and look back with a different goal in mind. You see, *reflection is where we begin the transformation in our hearts from fear of the future to trust in the One who holds it.*

He's always there. He's always in the details. And when we find Him there, we realize that He truly does love us immensely and holds us close. And when we reflect on His faithfulness, we can begin to find rest in the truth that He always goes before us to prepare a way.

The truth is, I very much believe that it's important to pause and reflect on what God is moving, shifting, and changing in our hearts for three very specific reasons:

1. Encouragement

A pause for reflection is encouraging to my spirit.

God may be working through the hard right now. Maybe He is with you in the forgiveness process. Maybe He's helping you overcome the lies of shame.

Or maybe, you feel His touch in the painful process of learning to let go. But no matter what He's helping you heal today, no matter what phase of growth you're in, when you reflect on His unwavering presence during *every* season of the journey, it's encouraging to know that He is always there and we are never on this journey alone. He has faithfully shown us His touches all throughout. Maybe you have been hearing His voice. Maybe you have seen His love notes. But one thing is for sure… He is walking you through it and He's holding you, loving you, and providing for you. And here's the key…

Focusing on His faithfulness will give you the strength and encouragement to take the next step, and then the next. Looping back to the rearview mirror, to pause and reflect on His goodness, will remind you that He is with you and for you, always.

2. Documentation

A pause for reflection gives me the chance to document His miracles.

I love this part! Sometimes when we are in the trenches, we can't see the true scale of the miracles that are taking place in our hearts and in our lives. When we pause to reflect, we can see God's hands in so much. And that's when we can document His miracles! I'm a huge believer in documenting the entire process. As I have mentioned before, there are many times when God speaks to me and I jot down His words in my journal. But, reflection … That is where the real *power* hits the paper. When I reflect back on everything Jesus has done in a situation, in my heart, or in my life overall, I'm often overwhelmed by what I see.

It doesn't really matter how you document. I have notes in my Bible, notes in my journal, notes on my blog, and other places as well. It's completely up to you. But here's the second important key behind reflection...

As you look back and document the beautiful miracles that took place, the undeniable fruition of His promises and the incredible evidence of His presence in your life, it will truly deepen your understanding of His heart and the depth of His love for you. And spoiler alert: It's a lot!

3. Gratitude

A pause for reflection encourages us to be thankful and grateful for His guiding hand all throughout the process. Even in the hard, it encourages us to remember to give thanks for the blessings that He is pouring out in our lives.

You see, I know that it can be difficult to feel Him or see Him through the sheets of rain that you may be experiencing today, but if we take the time to reflect on His faithfulness and His goodness, we will be reminded that He never leaves us to face the darkness, the wilderness, or even the bathroom floor without Him. He is always there, in the big and the small, in the seen and in the unseen, blessing you and guiding you.

So, how does the rearview mirror help our head bone

and our heart bone to join forces, to commit to an action plan together in this difficult season that we are facing?

Easy, actually! As we reflect on His presence during our darkest seasons, we suddenly realize that He truly is the God who shows up, the God who stays, and the God who delivers. And He is the God who will never (*ever!*) abandon us or fail us in any storm.

And that revelation, alone, was the key for me.

You see, if I *choose* to use this knowledge to *take action* in my life, to make small steps daily to *anchor my thoughts* to these truths, then this shift in my head bone will have incredible and life-changing effects on my heart!

In essence, here is the reason why I always loop myself back to the rearview mirror when I feel the most alone or afraid during a difficult season:

Reflection leads to clarity and an understanding of His presence, His touch, and His love in *all* situations and at *all* times.
↓

That understanding leads to a deepening of our relationship with Him and our trust in Him and His plans for us, solidly anchoring our heart to His.
↓

Our deeply personal relationship with Him gives us the courage and strength to *change* behavioral patterns, such as painful and restricting thought-processes.

↓

Changing these thought patterns, exchanging them with His truths, allows us to fully experience the outpouring of His love, peace, hope, joy, and rest.

↓

Fully experiencing the outpouring of His heart continually leads us into a deeper and more personal relationship with Him and an even greater understanding of His heart, which further reinforces and securely anchors our heart (and our faith and trust) to Him.

In other words, reflection has the power to spark a never-ending flow between my spirit and His. This life-changing flow renews my strength and hope and encourages change in my processing and patterns, allowing the full flow of His healing and love to reach my heart.

I encourage you today, take time to pause and truly reflect. Reflect on His love. Reflect on His guidance. Reflect on how His hand has never left you and His heart has always held you close. Reflect on what He is teaching you and speaking into you. And then take a moment, look in the rearview mirror, and document your miracles today.

He's an amazing Father and He loves you very much.

No matter the season, whether you are facing a storm or find yourself basking in the warmth of a beautiful day, He is ever-present, and when we pause to reflect, we can see His touch in every aspect of our lives. And that reassurance will pour hope, courage, peace and rest into our hearts, today.

In The Every Day

But what if we are not in this deeply painful head bone and heart bone cycle? How does this filtering process apply to our everyday lives and not just our healing? What if, in reflection, we find that our thoughts are often taking us down paths that we know are unhealthy?

The truth is, the *actions* that we *choose* to take in our daily lives, and not just in our difficult seasons, still have great influence over what is allowed to take root in our heart and how it feeds our spirit!

You see, when we strive to no longer sit in thoughts of anger, resentment, boasting, jealousy, or negativity towards each other, it has tremendous power. And let me just add, all that other stuff is heavy. Very, very heavy. When you can release it from your heart, the freedom and joy that you will begin to feel is truly life-changing. Let me share an example from my own journey...

Some years back, I was deeply hurt by a friend. Every time I thought of that friend, I would dwell on the hurt this person had caused. I would review the situation in my mind, playing it back like a movie reel. And even worse, each time I saw them, my heart would squeeze with unforgiveness, anger, and resentment.

When God confronted me about my thought patterns and my unforgiveness, I started to actively try to change my approach to the situation. For instance, when this person would enter my mind, I would not allow myself to dwell on what had happened, but rather, I would think to myself, "I forgive you and I hope that you are having a beautiful day and doing well." And I won't lie. It wasn't always easy. Honestly, sometimes the anger and the unforgiveness *feels* easier, on the lips and the heart, but what I found was that by changing my thought patterns, I began to truly change my heart towards that person.

After a while, I could see them in the grocery store and all of the old wounds began to feel like distant memories. I found that my heart actually smiled at them. Yes, my heart, and not just my face. And inside, I began to feel pure joy at the weight that had been lifted off *my* spirit.

But while this is an honest example, I also realize that it could be quite oversimplified for your situation. Your hurt may run much deeper or the circumstances may be much more complicated. In fact, your situation may not look like my example at all. Your new thought pattern may be something along the lines of…

"This person hurt me, but I won't dwell on it. I have created a healthy boundary where needed and then I gave the situation to Jesus. I will not allow my *thoughts* to drag me into a replay of the situation. I will not let (*insert negative feeling*) root further in my heart."

And that's okay.

In some situations, controlling your thoughts may be achieved through creating boundaries. In others, you may lay it at His feet again and again, over and over, as you work towards forgiveness so that *your* heart can heal. Each situation could (*and will*) be different, but the main thing here is that you guard your heart, be intentional about what you are watering in your mind, ask the Holy Spirit to help you realign when you find yourself in the less-than-ideal lane, and just continually grow in your peace and joy with Jesus.

Thought patterns are a challenging and yet necessary thing to address in our lives and on our journey to joy. It may be a funny play on words, but truly, the head bone *is* connected to the heart bone. Whatever we nurture, whatever we allow to take up space, whatever we water and proclaim, will most assuredly affect us mentally, emotionally, and spiritually on this journey.

Deeply Difficult Seasons

But what if reflection, though powerful and reassuring, just isn't enough to calm my debilitating thoughts of fear, anxiety, and hopelessness? What if I'm facing a deeply difficult season and I'm still staring at my mountain and feeling completely overwhelmed? And what if capturing those thoughts before they spiral my broken heart into defeat just feels absolutely impossible?

The truth is, it was often during my most difficult seasons when my head bone and my willpower to protect my heart bone would clash in a painful, ugly, and soul-crushing battle.

My head bone would work overtime trying to calculate every risk, think through all the what-ifs, and figure out all the ways to maintain full control of the situation and most importantly, prevent further damage. My willpower, on the other hand, would desperately wage war against these defeating thought patterns because I knew that they were drowning my heart bone in fear, anxiety, and hopelessness instead of anchoring my peace in God's plan for me.

You see, it's not that I didn't believe in the powerful truth behind the connection between my head and my heart, but when I would find myself absolutely drowning in joy-restricting thoughts, leading my heart to spiral into feelings of utter panic and pain, I simply *didn't know how* to take back the control... *any of it.*

And that's why this part of the chapter is here...

Because I wanted to reassure you that you are not alone and again, there is *not* something wrong with you (*oh, how I needed to hear that, at times!*). You are navigating through a very painful and difficult season and it's okay to *not* be okay.

And I want to give you hope as well... There will be a

better tomorrow. God is working in your situation right now. And while some of this chapter, and this journey, may deeply challenge you at times, here is the truth to which you can securely anchor your determination in even the most difficult moments...

If you speak life into His promises and let them motivate you to dig deeper into your healing, if you continually pray over the process and let God move through it, when you eventually break through that life-restricting and joy-obstructing wall of defeating and debilitating thoughts...

It will beautifully and indescribably set your heart free!

Now, I'm going to pause for a moment and be completely honest and transparent here...

Even though I know that joy does not come passively, that navigating the process of healing depends heavily on my willingness to be responsible for what I water in my thoughts and how it feeds my spirit, sometimes in my most difficult seasons, it all just seemed so completely *out of my control.* Heavy, even. Very, very heavy. And worse, trying to reign it in began to feel like another job, another burden, on my already grieving heart... and another failure.

Please hear my heart ... I am absolutely *not* trying to encourage or expect something of you that, at times, I felt too broken to achieve myself. I'm not here to minimize your processing or to give you another *overly-simplified* answer to your pain or fear. I'm only hoping that this part of the chapter will provide you with some encouragement for the journey ahead and some tools to take those first few steps. So, let's jump in...

The Resolution

I would first like to invite you today to *make a resolution that you will begin to apply a healthier filtering process with your thoughts.*

This doesn't mean that change will happen overnight, nor does it mean that all of your thoughts will be joyful or happy. It simply means that if the thought serves your spirit well, water it. And, if the thought harms your spirit and your heart, find the root. If it is rooted in unresolved anger, pain, resentment, or jealousy, pray over it and let God show you how to uproot it and replace it with something healthier.

It's a resolution, not a commitment to perfection.

It's making the decision that you don't want to stay in this place, you don't want to plant roots in this painful cycle, and you are committing to set your eyes (and your thoughts) on where He is taking you, over and over, until you get there.

Pray For Discernment

Once you've made that resolution, I encourage you to pray over it, daily. Ask God to give you discernment over your thoughts. Allow the Holy Spirit to give you divine wisdom and insights so that you may more easily navigate through this part of healing.

The truth is, sometimes in the tightly woven knots of pain, we *cannot* clearly see what is actually serving our spirit and what is harming it. And sometimes, we feel justified and we hold onto things that we know do not serve us well. Sometimes we carry anger and unforgiveness in our lives to give us "thicker skin" so that this kind of pain doesn't happen to us again. But we have to lay it *all* at His feet and ask Him what is serving our heart and what is breaking it. Because the truth is He can pour peace and strength into us that will help us plant our feet on a solid ground and create healthy spiritual, physical, and emotional boundaries *without* carrying those heavy and painful reminders that break us.

Discernment. Pray over it. Listen for His guidance. And if He shows you a source of harm in your thoughts or thought processes, let Him move through it and heal it. Don't hold onto things that are blocking you from the fulfillment of His peace and joy.

Processing Your Pain

Next, and very importantly, *seek out a way (or ways) to process your pain.* Don't deny it. Give it the space it needs and don't compare it, or your process, to others. If I can, I'd like to share with you a few ways that I learned to process my pain during my journey:

First, I'd like to highly (*highly*) recommend professional counseling. But please also hear my heart on this subject... Not all counselors are the perfect fit for all people. I encourage you to find one that makes you feel safe. Find one that challenges you in growth, but also encourages your heart and makes you feel heard and understood, valued, special, and important. If your counseling isn't helping you grow, or is leaving you feeling lost, hurt, hopeless, or misunderstood, it may not be the right fit for you. Pray over direction and ask God to bring the right counselor or therapist into your life.

Secondly, I recommend finding a way to express your thoughts and emotions. Journaling is a great option for many and it takes many different forms. I personally enjoy art journaling. For me, drawing became a great way to work through my feelings in an attempt to better understand the root causes. In a season of raw and intense emotions, it helped me to take pause in my reaction in order to process what I truly wanted to say. In the beginning, I kept my journal near me at all times. The time spent drawing out my thoughts and feelings often allowed just enough of a gap to take back control, calm my heart, pray, decide what I wanted to do with the thought or feeling (*water it or continue to pray over it*) and resume my day accordingly. But finding a healthy way to express or work through your thoughts and emotions can take many different forms. Exercise, art, writing, dancing, music, walking, and running are all great ways to take a pause. Finding what works for you is definitely the key.

Third, *share your journey with people that you feel safe and comfortable with and ask them to pray over you.* I cannot even begin to express how much this helped me. Remember, I'm the girl that kept everyone and everything at arm's length. I had a *very* (*very*) small community of close friends and family that knew what I was going through, but when I finally opened up to them, their encouraging words, messages of love when they were just checking in, and constant prayers over me always looped me back to the headspace that I wanted to be in. In some ways, they kept me accountable. You see, when my head bone would begin to spiral, they would remind me who I was and where He was taking me. And all we have to do is loop back to chapter nine to know why their prayers meant so much. We were never meant to carry it alone.

Here's the truth: God will give you divinely placed people to walk the road with you and pray over you.

Lastly, but most importantly, *take it to your Father.* He is so good and so faithful. He does not seek perfection. He knows your pain. And He desires to give you a more joyful rhythm in your heart. Cry out to Him. Ask Him to lift you; to meet you where you are and pour out His love over you. Whether you need encouragement and reassurance, discernment over a thought, or help to overcome a thought process or behavior, He will be there.

And just to wrap this chapter up with one final encouraging food-for-thought note to give you hope during this part of your journey...

When I know that I'll never be alone, that He will never

leave me, abandon me, or fail me, I suddenly feel *safe* and I can find rest.

When I know that He believes in me, cares for me, loves me, is truly for me, and has already equipped me, I suddenly feel stronger and I find courage.

When I realize that He is the God who shows up, the God who stays, and the God who holds me through even the roughest storms, I suddenly feel the fear and the anxiety begin to melt away, replaced by His peace.

And when I realize the true depth of His love for me, I suddenly find myself able to face tomorrow, to face my next chapter, even in the storms, because I know that any journey or path He lays before me is littered with His blessings and, best of all, will be walked hand in hand with Him!

Give Him this battle over your head bone and your heart bone and continue to lean into Him. He will see you through.

Chapter 18

God Doesn't Make Mistakes

I think it's about time for a super uplifting feel-good chapter, don't you? And I just love (*LOVE!*) this chapter because even in the straightforward simplicity of its message, it absolutely hits my heart in all the perfect happy places! Believe it! Let it deeply root into your spirit! God doesn't ever (*ever, ever*) make mistakes!

...

Last Saturday while sweating my way through spin class with a few other ladies, I found myself telling the fun, but embarrassing story about *that one time* my husband decided to take me to a fancy vineyard in Canada. Now, I'm just a simple, small town country girl. I usually talk too loud and too much. I definitely wear my heart on my sleeve and my feelings on my face. My idea of comfort beverages are coffee and sweet tea, preferably enjoyed while sitting in a rocking chair on a front porch somewhere. And well, as this story requires me to share, I also happen to occasionally enjoy a bottle of cheap sparkling apple cider. Which loops me back to the vineyard...

When the sommelier (*I had to look that word up*) asked me about my wine preferences, I probably shouldn't have just blurted out that my absolute favorite way to drink wine is half a glass of wine and half a glass of cheap sparkling apple cider. I kid you not... he moved down the bar and never came back. (*But... it's just soooo good!*) Anyways, just as I'm finishing telling these ladies in spin class my funny story, I hear something absolutely beautiful roll out of my mouth and it instantly stops me in my tracks...

"But you know, I'm just me. And that's all I want to be."

And guess what? I meant it. In fact, when my brain did a double-take, questioning if my words were genuine, my heart did a little jig because I suddenly realized that this little (BIG) admission came from some place deep inside. Some place that had traveled through a tremendous amount of healing to arrive here. Some place that had been touched very deeply by a God that loves me more than I could have ever comprehended. And suddenly, I wanted to hop off that bike and dance, right there in the middle of spin class!

As you know by now, I have spent my entire life trying to fit everyone's mold; trying to be accepted, approved, and loved by everyone. But over the course of the last year, I've been slowly learning that one of the most beautiful things that God can teach us during our journey, during *your* journey, is that He does not ever (*ever, ever!*) make mistakes.

When He made me.

When He made you.

When He decided on our gifts.

When He designed our calling.

When He chose to love us.

When He gave us grace.

When He called us beautiful, chosen, and His.

They weren't mistakes then and they aren't mistakes now, no matter what road we have traveled. He meant it then. And He still does today. *All of it.*

You see, here's the key that took me a long time to accept... I *could not* fully embrace His beautiful and perfect calling for my life without *first* letting go of what everyone else could (*or would*) think of me!

What a Noah moment, right? Or moments, I should say, because He has patiently guided me through this understanding, reminding me over and over that I am His and He delights in me, just as I am. And He delights in you, too.

Loud or Quiet.

Introvert or Extrovert.

Homebody or Adventure Seeker.

Silly or Serious.

Neat Freak or Messy.

Right-Brain or Left-Brain Dominant.

Super Chill or a Little Extra.

Wine Connoisseur or just a simple country girl who really likes cheap sparkling apple cider.

You are IRREPLACEABLE in His eyes.

You are one-of-a-kind. Beautiful and incredible!

He skillfully and intentionally crafted every single amazing thing that makes you... *you*.

You have a purpose that you are specifically designed to fulfill. A plan that is for you alone. A calling that is only on your heart. And you, my friend, are...

THE perfect fit.

Ever feel like you're not really good at, or made for, anything? Yeah... Me too! But see, here's the undeniable truth that outshines those defeating thoughts and feelings...

Our faithful and loving Father is *the* master architect, *the* master artist, and He has flawlessly designed us to be precisely fitted for His plan!

Irreplaceable... Yes, you...

You are irreplaceable to Him!

And I'll say it again... He doesn't make mistakes.

Ever. Ever, Ever.

And friends, He's inviting us to dance in the absolute freedom of this message today!

He's asking us to bring our doubts to Him so that He can help us break through the chains of insecurity and fear because here's His unshakeable promise to us:

There's no distance we can run or feeling we can throw at Him to *ever* change His mind. He loves you the same yesterday, today, and tomorrow. We may change. We may travel through difficult seasons and make mistakes or even grow angry at Him, but *He* will never be shaken. His love for you will *never* change.

The steadfast love of the LORD never ceases; his mercies never come to an end; they are new every morning; great is your faithfulness. (Lamentations 3:22-23 ESV)

Your calling is not a mistake.

His faith in you is not a mistake.

His never-ending love and grace for you is not a mistake.

And your incredibly unique design was not, nor will ever be, a mistake. In fact, your very being was meticulously and carefully planned down to every last intimate and intricate beautiful detail by the One who loves you most!

"My child, you are so beautiful to me. I delight in you. I'm captivated by you. I deeply, deeply cherish you. I love to hear your laugh. I love to see your smile. You are my absolute prized possession. And you are so incredibly irreplaceable to me."

Believe it. Receive it. And let it deeply root in your heart, today. He loves you, individually. So much! And He doesn't ever (ever, ever!) make mistakes!

So shine bright, my friends!

Be the incredible you, today!

Chapter 19

Identifying Your Links

*Never doubt God's mighty power to work in you and
accomplish all this. He will achieve infinitely more
than your greatest request, your most unbelievable
dream, and exceed your wildest imagination.*
(Ephesians 3:20 TPT)

I made a trip to our local grocery store recently just to
grab a few things. Since school was out for the
summer, the store was full of little kids tagging along
with mom and dad, venturing up and down the aisles
with true childlike enthusiasm. Two little girls in
particular caught my attention that day. They were
holding hands, hopping along and loudly sharing big
stories with each other, voices full of excitement and
the occasional giggles. I smiled at them and they didn't
hesitate to flash a big smile in return. And I immediately
recognized something in their eyes… Joy. Childlike joy.

Their happiness made my heart skip with delight and
then it made my spirit take pause to question, what is

it that changes us through the years? What happens in that gap between childhood and middle age? Why do so many of us find ourselves truly struggling to flash a genuine and sincere heartfelt smile when someone greets us? Are we tired? Yes, absolutely. Are we overwhelmed and stressed? Most definitely. Does our to-do list seem daunting in every aspect of life? No doubt. But it just felt like there had to be more to it.

And then it painfully dawned on me...

Life just knocks it right out of us, doesn't it?

Jobs, friendship, motherhood, marriage, health, finances... it can all be so challenging at times. Difficult and painful seasons inevitably find us all until one day we wake up and realize that we no longer *feel* childlike joy anymore. And worse, we resign ourselves to the fact that this is just the reality of adulthood. Welcome to the real world! Joy is reserved for the days of childhood and then life teaches you better, right? In fact, we've almost come to expect the joy-robbing blows and lows because well... *that's just life.*

And sometimes I wonder what you think when you read the title of this book, A Time to Dance: Chasing Joy in Difficult Seasons? Do you think that it's possible to return to childlike joy or do you think that by the time we reach adulthood we are all too defeated, and possibly too broken, to ever truly dance again?

I used to think the latter. I used to think that adulthood was littered with realities that inevitably led to broken spirits and broken hearts. I grew to believe that expecting otherwise would be completely naïve, resulting in a more painful, humiliating, and dramatic fall. But then, in my most difficult season, when I had resigned myself to this way of life the most, Jesus stepped into my pain and spoke these very important words over my heart...

"Your life and your story will not be defined by this season, my child. I will not only restore your joy, but I will fill it up until your cup overflows."

And He will do the same for you.

...

I want to take a step back for a moment to that particular time in my healing journey and share a personal story with you. Remember the art journaling that I mentioned in chapter seventeen? I used it often in my healing when I had an emotion or thought and found myself needing to take a pause to process it and find its roots. I'll never forget one drawing in particular that seems to relate so closely to this topic...

In the drawing, I was standing next to the ocean. The sun was shining, but my body was in the shadows. I could see the sun, but I could not feel it's warmth. I could hear the ocean, but I couldn't dip my toes into its peaceful and cool touch. You see, I had chains wrapped around my ankles that held me back. Chains that kept me literally *just out of reach* of everything that I knew would lift my spirit. I was close enough to see it and know it was there, but too far away to truly feel it in my heart. Even more frustrating and defeating, I was held back by *something* that I couldn't identify.

And how many of us can relate to this? Seeing the warmth. Seeing the joy. Seeing peace, happiness, and delight. We know it's right there. In fact, we can feel ourselves right on the cusp, but somehow, we just can't quite tap into it. We just can't seem to break free of these chains.

If you feel that way today, then this chapter is written for you. Because when we find ourselves in this space, it's easy to begin to wonder if we are somehow failing; that as we journey through these chapters, we're just missing something. Or maybe, it's because the damage done by someone else's choices or mistakes have chained us to this feeling of utter brokenness forever, just out of reach of experiencing all that God is pouring out.

I know firsthand how our minds often work overtime to search and identify the cause of our just-out-of-reach feelings and thoughts. We reason that if we can understand it and dissect it, then we can put a plan in place to overcome it. And though we try so hard to solve and rectify the problem of what's missing ourselves, when that doesn't work, it can be even more frustrating to our already confused and hurting hearts.

And it is in times like these that it becomes painfully easy to begin to resign ourselves to the shadows...

This is just how it is for me. Joy is reserved for someone else, possibly for someone else reading this very book, but not for me.

Friends, as I write those words, I can't help but feel an ache in my heart. I, too, have felt the painful and powerful defeat of accepting the idea that healing and joy were just *too* out of reach for *someone like me*. And, let me gently warn you, the enemy is beyond satisfied when we stop right there. Defeated and done. Setting the book down, setting our journey down, and walking away.

But then, *there's Jesus*!

If you're feeling this confusion and pain today, I just invite you to open your heart to the next part of this chapter and here's why...

God's voice and His touch can identify and break through every link that holds you captive in the shadows and the truth is that He desires nothing more than to set you free!

You see, after my own painful season of peeling back the layers, trying to identify what was holding me back, I came to realize one beautiful truth that allowed me to finally find peace and rest...

I didn't *need* to have it all figured out on my own. I just needed to take my chain to Jesus and ask Him to help me sort through it little by little, link by link, until I was completely set free.

And He met me there. Right where I was. And we began the work *together.*

Let me explain...

If it seems like my story of healing and chasing joy was a step-by-step process, that's because it really was. As I laid my chain at His feet and started praying over it, I rested in the promise that *His timing and His process* for healing was far better than anything that I could plan for myself. And that's when He, quite literally, started revealing, healing, and breaking through my chain *one link at a time,* slowly and intricately.

This went on for months, years even. Every chapter of this book was another link, and as they broke, one by one, I could feel more warmth, more joy, reaching my heart. And yet, in His infinite wisdom, *the pace remained slow*, gentle enough that I could manage to face each link with Him, revisiting old scars, insecurities, and things that attacked my heart, without feeling overwhelmed by my entire chain all at once.

I won't lie. I sometimes grew impatient and wanted to experience all the breakthroughs right away, but His timing was intentionally steady and unhurried as He took me through each step on the journey - releasing my shame, facing my struggles with perfectionism, giving Him my fears, and on and on. We journeyed through so many things that held me back; things that I struggled to understand or overcome. And as I would feel one link break, He would lovingly reveal the next

"Your life and your story will not be defined by this season, my child.

I will not only restore your joy, but I will fill it up until your cup overflows."

link as we walked through the work and healing together, day after day. And friends, here's the truth: He is still working on my links, even today. So, hear my heart on this...

You're over halfway through this book and I'm deeply and sincerely praying for you. Praying that you are beginning to see and maybe even feel the warmth of joy on your face. But I'm also guessing that, like me, there may still be some things keeping you from experiencing the fullness of it.

We all have different links, different stories, different pain, and your chain may look very different than mine. Today, I just encourage you to take your chain to Jesus and ask Him to help reveal it and work through it, to guide you step-by-step into your healing, and then trust in the pace of His timing.

He promises to pour out joy over each one of us. And not just a little, but cup-overflowing childlike joy! And I firmly believe in the fulfillment of His promises. The enemy would like nothing more than for us to feel exhausted and resign ourselves to the fact that joy is for someone else – someone less hurt or someone who has made less mistakes; someone whose heart is not as bruised and broken or someone that has more faith. But if we listen closely, Jesus is right there saying, "Trust me. I am here. And I will see you through."

Take your chain to Him. His loving hand will guide you through it one step at a time. And with each step, each broken link, you'll feel the warmth entering those deep and once-dormant parts of your spirit and heart, again. *Those are His promises.*

I'd like to end this chapter with the same verse that we started with. Believe it to be true for your life and your heart today…

Never doubt God's mighty power to work in you and accomplish all this. He will achieve infinitely more than your greatest request, your most unbelievable dream, and exceed your wildest imagination.
(Ephesians 3:20 TPT)

Chapter 20

Through His Lenses

As you journey through this chapter, you'll find that it gracefully ties into some of what we discussed in chapter sixteen. But it's also a beautiful and freeing truth that deserves a deeper dive into one very important and relevant concept that God has recently been laying heavily on my heart. My friends, though it's challenging at times, if you press into this message, I think you'll find that it will truly bless you!

....

If you have ever looked through someone else's prescription glasses, you know that it can quickly turn your vision into one big blurry mess. My husband and I both wear glasses and we also happen to have the exact same frames, so you can imagine that when we occasionally grab the wrong ones, it takes about a sum total of half a second to realize our mistake because our prescription is nowhere close to the same. We literally can't see anything clearly when we try looking through the wrong lenses. And there is so much value,

214

so much to be learned, from that one very important concept.

You see, as God has been walking me through my own healing and joy journey over the last year, I have frequently felt Him speaking to me about *my* lenses versus *His* lenses.

Sometimes it relates to the reflection in the bathroom mirror. As He has been teaching me to see myself the way that He sees me, the healing from that beautiful and life-giving concept has been an invaluable and very important part of my journey.

Likewise, He sometimes changes things up and challenges me to apply this message when looking at the hearts of others. And when I have truly listened and leaned into this part of the process, I have always found myself equally blessed. Why? Because God knows that when we view people through His lenses, or as closely as we can, it has the power to completely change our perspective and move us towards more compassion, grace, humility and empathy.

And He knows that changing our perspective has the healing power to free our hearts.

The truth is, even when we strive to choose prayer over judgment in our lives, it's often all-too-easy to see a friend, a loved one, a co-worker, or an acquaintance making one confusing and hurtful decision after another and find ourselves thinking, *"What's wrong with them?"* The answer to that question is usually followed up with a lot of judgment and we often justify or reason that our perspective on the situation is both warranted and valid.

But maybe that family member or friend is going through something really difficult and they are scared, running, and deeply hurting. Maybe that coworker has a heavy emotional scar that they want so badly to heal from but they truly don't know how. Maybe the enemy is tormenting that acquaintance with lies and keeping their heart chained and imprisoned in a defeating and painful cycle of destruction...

That doesn't mean that every night when they rest their head on the pillow, God isn't speaking directly to their heart and saying, "*My child, I'm right here. I love you. I will never leave you.*"

Remember, God has never asked us to clean ourselves up or pull ourselves together so that we could rise up high enough to be worthy of His presence and love. No. The beautiful truth is that Jesus came down and met us, right where we were, and wrapped Himself gently around our broken hearts until we let go of everything else that we carried and found healing at His feet.

And here is the challenge...

If our incredible Heavenly Father is meeting them with that same unwavering and unconditional love, the very same grace that He so often poured over us during this journey, who am I to judge them with anything else?

You see, God knows their hearts. He sees their pain. He knows exactly what roads they have traveled and what decisions they have made, and hear this... He shows up and He stays, an unwavering presence in their lives, working in the details, reminding them who they are in Him and how much they are loved. And thank you, Jesus, for doing the same for me, over and over again.

His lenses instead of mine... A complete perspective change.

Perhaps the hardest lesson in this concept is when God taps my heart about the person that I still struggle to forgive. Yes, on my path to joy, I still struggle to forgive. But, in those times when I feel my heart beginning to spiral in judgment, God patiently and lovingly reminds me, *"Remember, my child, I love them the same..."*

But, how can you, God? They have been mean, manipulative, and are clearly not walking a path chasing your heart. It's not okay how they chose to hurt me. And God, they don't even feel remorse or seek forgiveness. Doesn't that make them unworthy? (*My unforgiveness on clear display.*)

But, though the hurt in me sometimes fights to resist His words, God's response never wavers. *He loves them the same. Yes, the same. The same... as me.* And it's a beautiful promise and piece of our Father's heart that I have grown to truly love and deeply appreciate.

You see, His heart breaks at their choices, just as His heart sometimes breaks at mine. I *am not* somehow more worthy, more special, or more cherished. No, He calls them His. Yes, His. All the same.

And if I'm being completely honest, sometimes the unforgiveness in me resists that truth. Greatly. You see, I'm not interested in the part of "religion" where I claim or pretend to walk in nothing but love, perfect forgiveness, and grace. No... I struggle sometimes, especially where there are deep scars present. And I'm willing to bet that, if we're honest, you do too.

But, you see, no matter how I struggle to understand or accept, *it's still not about my lenses*... It's about His.

The truth is, when I pause to look through His lenses, I am momentarily moved to compassion at what brokenness in their lives must have led them to these confusing and destructive choices. And as this concept begins to deeply root in my heart, the shift in my perspective moves me to take action. I find myself beginning to take small steps each day to change my approach, to change my patterns of unhealthy assumptions and judgement. I begin to try to view their hearts, their actions, and their choices through His lenses of love and grace instead of mine, even in the most difficult of circumstances. Make that e*specially* in the most difficult circumstances.

But in reflecting on that change in my own life, I've found that one of the most rewarding parts about looking through His lenses instead of my own is that it has also led my heart to release so many toxic space-savers: Judgment, resentment, anger, shame, and unforgiveness. Individually, they are heavy enough to do some real destruction to my heart, but when combined, their impact is truly crushing. Alternately, when we choose to view through His lenses of love and grace, it brings us that much closer to finding true peace and lasting joy; it opens those spaces in our hearts to His outpouring of something that is so much better.

And there is one more added bonus that our Father loves about this choice, this action on our part: Choosing to forgive, having empathy, giving grace, and allowing His healing to pour through our anger and resentment also *makes us an incredible witness for His heart.* He will use our compassion, grace, love, and willingness to change our perspective to speak into others about the healing powers of Jesus.

In other words, if we are willing to make the choice to lean into this growth, it opens our hearts to deep healing *and* gives us the opportunity to lift others along the way. And that's a win, win in my book!

I invite you, today, to commit to trying on a new set of lenses. *When you feel judgment entering your thoughts, your heart, your actions, or your words, commit to a pause, whenever you can, and try to view the situation through God's lenses. It's not about perfection. It's about progress.* But, the more we put this idea into practice, the more our hearts will naturally move towards compassion, love, and grace.

And remember, making the choice in your heart doesn't mean that a noticeable change will always be easy or immediate. I'm not here to pretend that it is. But when it's really difficult to see the person or situation through His lenses, that's when we just take it to Him and lay it at His feet. When our supply feels tapped and our limits feel stretched, our faithful Father promises to pour His divine power into the situation and blanket our hearts.

I'm learning with you today. The key is commitment and growth. We are in this together! It's not about our lenses... it's about His.

Chapter 21

Your Qualifications for His Kingdom's Work

One night last spring, after the rest of my little family had long gone to sleep, I found myself up late reading in bed. There was nothing innately special or unique about this night, but it was about to be. You see, as I closed the book, preparing to tuck in, I suddenly heard God speak to my heart…

"I want you to write a book."

I think I may have actually laughed out loud. I can clearly remember my immediate reaction and somewhat argumentative response…

"Write a book? God, no way! What do I have to offer? I'm nothing special. Nothing at all. A hot mess and total disaster. What can I possibly contribute that would make a difference? And, PS… with what time?"

I'm not really sure what I expected Him to say, but I can

tell you with one hundred percent certainty that I *definitely* didn't expect everything that transpired next…

Like the patient Father that He is, God just let the discussion hang in the air between us. His gentle nudge. My stubborn push back. He made no further attempt to discuss the matter with me that night. Satisfied that I had made a solid and indisputable argument on my end, I fell asleep shortly after our little one-sided tiff.

Sometimes people ask me how I've grown to trust that I'm hearing God's voice. Well, He occasionally takes me on a wild ride with His fingerprints unquestionably all over the road map as confirmation of His calling. And this, my friends, was definitely one of those moments!

When I woke up the next morning, I had a text message on my phone from someone in my life that, for completely unrelated reasons, I had shared a blog post with earlier that week. The message sitting on my phone included the following line…

"*I think you have a book in you.*"

Coincidence? Yes… and yet, *not random at all*. A total God moment.

I kid you not… At this point, I *know* I laughed out loud. *Okay, God. I'm listening. Sorry for arguing. But for the record, I still think you're crazy. PS, God… with what time?*

The next week, I received a call and it was the final and last confirmation that I needed to let go of my reservations, fears, doubts, and arguments and simply take the step of faith that He was calling me to make. You see, the call was from my department chair and she was relaying an important update regarding my job at the college. I would not be needed in my adjunct instructor position for the upcoming semester because they had interviewed and hired a full-time instructor to cover all adjunct classes. I was free to explore other options for the time being.

Well, alright, God. Fine. We will do this your way.

And friends, hear my testimony and my heart… You're reading that very book today. He is an amazing (and patient) Father.

I like to think that God doesn't mind that this is how our relationship goes sometimes. His gentle nudge. My resistant push back. His gentle nudge. A heel or two dug into my comfort zone. His gentle nudge. My final shrug and laugh of understanding and acceptance. I imagine Him saying something along the lines of…

"Oh, my stubborn child, I do love you."

I love you too, God. Thank you for being my friend.

What Are Your Qualifications?

If you travel a bit further back in my story, or a few chapters back in this book, you will see that a huge turning point in my journey was when I asked God to use me ... like really, really use me. After He had so patiently walked me through a great deal of healing and blanketed me with grace, love, forgiveness, and encouragement, I was eager to find His calling on my life and share His heart with others. However, as I reflect on many of the big moments when He opened doors and invited me to step out in faith, there seems to be a common underlying message in my initial response.

Over and over, I argued with Him...

I am nothing special. I have nothing special to offer. How could I possibly contribute anything of value? I don't think I have the right spiritual gifts for what you're asking. I won't know the right words to say. What if I get this all wrong? What if I completely let you down?

And what I'm really arguing is ...

Don't you want to use someone else, God? Someone with more qualifications? Someone who has proven that they can handle the task? Someone who can assure you that they will get the job done right?

But again and again, He confirms...

I want you.

What are your qualifications? It's one of the first things that an employer asks during an interview. And, it's one of the first things I ask myself when God taps my heart.

But God doesn't question my qualifications. He's not asking me to list off all the jobs I've gotten right; the times I've scored the goal; all the moments that I've absolutely nailed it for Him. And He's definitely not persuaded by my list of all the reasons that I'm the wrong person for the task. He is not going to suddenly have an "aha" moment and tell me I have been so completely right all along. I'm a terrible choice, after all. The absolute worst option. The last (backup to the backup) draft pick. No...

His still small voice is unwavering as it meets my heart with the same message each time...

I choose you.

You see, my qualifications have never mattered. My faith in Him and my willingness to follow His lead is all He desires.

I hear Him calling to me today...

"Run with me, child!"

And here's the thing, I can't help but notice that punctuation at the end of His calling. In truth, my heart lifts because I know that He means it. He intentionally and emphatically placed an exclamation point there. Which leads me to take action. Why? Because I can't let the enemy place a question mark where God has already placed His unwavering love and faith in me.

I do not know the calling that God has placed on your heart, but today I invite you to see yourself as not only chosen, but a perfect fit, regardless of your qualifications. When we ask God to use us, we are trusting that He will provide everything that we need. And here's *His truth*: He will!

There is so much joy to be found in leaning into God's plan for your life. He has placed a calling on your heart just for you and nobody else. He never leaves your side and His calling does not change because you travel through a dry season or weather a heart-breaking and, possibly faith-shattering, storm.

He doesn't seek perfection. Remember, YOU are irreplaceable in the Kingdom and the exact fit for the position. Don't worry about your qualifications. He will meet you right where you are.

Oh... and about that adjunct instructor position that I lost in the moving and shaking of His plans.... Well, one week after I mailed out this book to a select group of editors for final reviews, I received a call completely out of the blue...

My dream college...

The college that had inspired me to be an instructor to begin with...

The college that I had not contacted for at least a year or more…

The very college with which I had prayed for an opportunity to teach at for years…

…was suddenly and unexpectedly on the other end of the line…

We would like for you to join our family. We would like for you to teach for us.

And there it was.

The tears poured.

A future more incredible than I had even dreamed for myself anymore.

There it was.

But, Jesus!

He is a good, good Father and you are His perfect fit. He has never cared about your qualifications for His Kingdom's work. He cares about your heart. *And He will see you through to a more beautiful future than even you can dream for yourself!*

Follow His nudges, let go of your self-doubt, trust in His provisions, and run with Him today!

Chapter 22

Have Faith, Stay the Course

I've ran a few spiritual marathons in my personal life, but it is with my husband's blessing that I share the story of this very personal marathon –

A few years ago, my husband traveled through a season of very painful mourning and our little family struggled. *Deeply* struggled. Grief and trauma are very, very difficult roads, as many of you know, and the depression, confusion, and anger overwhelmed him in waves until he felt completely consumed by it. Though we tried so hard to be there for him, we quickly found ourselves mourning our own loss, the loss of him. You see, he was physically still there, but emotionally he felt hollow, and the ripple effect on our family was painfully substantial and scary. This beautiful husband of mine remained a strong, hardworking, and dedicated professional by day, but at home he was struggling to hold it all together. *We* were struggling to hold it all together. And make no mistake, the enemy knew it too.

My best friend of twenty years quickly found himself in the biggest spiritual fight of his life, one that would change our family forever, and I felt completely powerless to help or control the outcome.

As I reflect back on that time in our lives, my heart still squeezes with emotions. I spent a year on my knees; a year feeling completely alone and absolutely terrified. I cried, I screamed, I begged, and I prayed, over and over again as I watched my husband toeing the edge of a cliff, all while tethered to the people he loved most, us. Where he went, we went. But despite the growing panic in my heart and my desperate attempts to reach him, the words that poured out of me and the tears that so often fell without warning had absolutely no power. He simply (and painfully) just could not see us.

A marathon season for sure… *but Jesus!*

Not a day goes by that I don't thank God for His faithfulness during that incredibly difficult season and for the grace and love that He poured into our journey of healing that followed. You see, our path to healing did not look the same, but God met both of us right where we were and He healed us, individually. And all of that is to say this…

Even if your situation or your miracle doesn't look the same, He *can* heal you too. And He will love you and hold you through it, whatever *it* is that you are facing today. Your healing and your future are safe in His hands. Look to Him first, above all else, and let Him be your guide.

The beautiful and life-giving truth that I learned in the middle of all that pain was that God is always at work, even when I cannot see it. That He can, and will, reach into our lives in a moment of pain, pour through us and heal our hearts. That our healing and our journey with Him is not dependent on anyone else's road to healing or actions, but rather is a very personal and intimate journey that exists between my heart and His. And that no matter what the next chapter brings, He can reweave our painful seasons into something that blesses us.

No matter the outcome, my friends, He will always remind us *every step of the journey* that we... *that you...* are His. And you are held by the One who loves you most.

So, before we dive deeper into this chapter, I'd like to pause for just a moment and say this...

No matter what marathon you face, or the outcome, He is in this. He is with you. And He will be faithful to bring you through.

...

Of all the marathons that I have encountered in my life, I think *my least challenging* was the actual 26.2 miles that I ran at the 2014 Little Rock Marathon. Hang with me here for a second because there is a beautiful lesson in this story that I just had to share...

If you happen to be familiar with the Little Rock Marathon, you know this particular year by heart. A powerful storm moved in, complete with dramatic temperature drops, sleet, extreme cold temps, and freezing winds. As we made our way past mile marker eighteen on the course, we were informed that they had shut down the race. Shuttles and buses were soon lining the roads escorting runners back. Race volunteers held signs along the path that read, "Large Hail Coming," "Seek Shelter," and "Event Canceled."

With tears in my eyes, I turned to my husband, an avid runner who had lovingly agreed to run my first marathon with me, and asked if he minded if we continued on. I doubted there would be a medal. Probably not any spectators or finish line photos. Maybe not even a true finish line. But I couldn't give up hope that there had to be something for my heart waiting at the end of this race.

To better explain my emotions that day, my decision to run a marathon came after our 4th round of fertility treatment and an extremely heartbreaking miscarriage. I wasn't sure if my heart could take any more pain or disappointment and I needed to be able to believe in something. So, I fixed my focus on a goal that I wanted so badly to accomplish and the journey became about so much more than the 26.2 miles or a medal. It was about healing. It was about restoration and hope. And as the elements around me raged that day, threatening to take me out of the race, I knew, deep down, that I needed to survive this storm. My heart needed me to make it through.

As I reflect back on the only physical marathon that I have ever ran, I'm realizing the parallels between what my husband and I encountered on that road and the marathons that we so often run in our spiritual lives.

Maybe you are in the middle of your own storm and God is calling your name. Maybe you aren't sure whether to turn back or press on. Maybe it hurts. *Really* hurts. But, if you pause, close your eyes, and listen, you'll hear His voice. He's reminding you of His promises. He's reminding you of His love. And He's reminding you that He will never leave you and He will see you through.

And friends, here is what He so beautifully reminded me that day...

When it seems like you are in pain and trudging through the hard while everyone else is reaching the joyful finish line...

Have faith. Stay the course.

When voices tell you to turn back, the storm is too big, the promise is gone, nothing is waiting for you at the finish line...

Have faith. Stay the course.

When the enemy tells you that you can't do this, you are not made for this, you don't have what it takes...

Have faith. Stay the course.

When it's so tempting to take the shuttle back to the start because your heart is broken, you've worked so hard, and it feels like nothing is going right...

Have faith. Stay the course.

Because you see, we did reach that finish line in 2014 and as we approached the big welcoming arch, I realized that there were no spectators left. No crowds cheering us on. No high-fives to congratulate us on making it through. But there was a finish line, complete with the promised medal. And more than that, there was healing. Following our marathon, my husband and I went on to have another heartbreak, a second failed IVF, before we were blessed with our beautiful miracle baby in 2015.

The truth is, sometimes when we are running the course of healing and the storms are building around us, threatening to take us out of the race, the only thing we have to hold onto is *His promise*. But in those moments, keep your eyes fixed on Him. The journey may be difficult. *It may not look like anybody else's.* You may be struggling to lift your feet and keep going. The enemy may be trying to tell you that you are not going to make it, my friends... but Jesus!

Run towards your healing. Run towards your joy and your hope in Him. Run towards His voice and His promises. Have faith. Trust Him. He loves you too much to watch you turn back. Rest in His arms when you need it, and when you're ready, stand up and run your race again.

Stay the course. Keep going. Keep faith... Because God is with you and He promises that you will not fail.

I pray with great faith for you, because I'm fully convinced that the One who began this gracious work in you will faithfully continue the process..."
(Philippians 1:6 TPT)

Chapter 23

Sitting in God's Waiting Room

After sharing the story of my family's very personal marathon in the last chapter, it seemed only fitting to share with you what God so lovingly taught me during that difficult season of sitting in His waiting room. I hope it blesses you, friends. My heart is with you in the wait.

...

In the Book of Psalms, chapter 69, David cries out,

"God, my God, come and save me! These floods of trouble have risen higher and higher. The water is up to my neck! I'm sinking into the mud with no place to stand, and I'm about to drown in this storm. I'm weary, exhausted with weeping. My throat is dry, my voice is gone, my eyes are swollen with sorrow, and I'm waiting for you, God, to come through for me."
(Psalm 69:1-3 TPT)

"I'm waiting for you, God, to come through for me."

The New Century Version translation reads the end of that passage as,

"I am tired from calling for help; my throat is sore." (Psalm 69:3)

"I am tired from calling for help…"

I have felt that, friends. All of it. And I know that you have too.

If we take another little hop, travel back a bit further in the Book of Psalms, you'll hear David asking God,

> *"I'm hurting, Lord… How much longer, Lord? Will You look the other way when I'm in need? How much longer must I cling to this constant grief? I've endured this shaking of my soul. So how much longer…"*
> (Psalm 13:1-2 TPT)

> *"Lord, how long will you watch this happen?"* (Psalm 35:17 NCV)

"How much longer, Lord? How much longer…"

God's waiting room. An often uncomfortable, and sometimes terrifying place when life gets truly difficult.

"I'm waiting for you, God. (Waiting for you…) to come through for me."

…

My husband and I have a marker board hanging on the wall in our bedroom. Whenever we have a family member or friend that is going through a challenging season... a storm, a big life change, an illness, a devastating divorce, a stressful move, or a painful loss... we add their name to the board. This is our way of committing to praying with them as they journey through the hard. Earlier today, as I paused and read through the names of many people that I love on that board, I came to realize one thing...

Like so many of us, they are all sitting in God's waiting room, prayerfully waiting for His answers and trusting in His timing, His guidance, and His provisions.

God's Waiting Room. It can be so incredibly difficult, especially in life-altering situations. When so much hangs in the balance, the unknowns can be almost unbearable. Fear can give rise to panic rather quickly. We know that our world may be irreversibly changed, but we feel completely out of control and helpless to direct the outcome. We can quite easily find ourselves in a cycle of anxiety, frustration, and even anger. You'll get no judgment from me. I have sat in God's waiting room and worked through every emotion mentioned. And trust me, God can handle it. But I'll probably never forget the season when He spoke into my heart and began to teach me how to stop pacing, stop panicking, stop fighting, and simply (yet, not so simply) lean in and start trusting.

You see, God is always present. In the chaos. In the

storm. In the hard. In the unbearable. In those moments when we release the most soul-wrenching and primal screams of pain. He's always at work in our lives. And He's so loving and so faithful. He could snap His fingers and give us exactly what we want, but in His infinite wisdom, He can often see what we truly need and there is so much blessing in trusting that.

Sometimes the waiting has a reason we don't understand, but make no mistake, we are always in His heart when He is keeping us there. So, that leads us to the question...

What can we do when we find ourselves in that space between our prayers and His answers?

Well, I have one humble suggestion and it has been a quite powerful tool for me when I find myself sitting in His waiting room...

Simply put, Be Ready.

Focus on your Heavenly Father and "*Be Ready*" to feel Him. I promise, He's there. And He is speaking into your heart, steadying you with His peace, love, and hope. Watch Him move in your situation. He will pour out His blessings in the middle of your storm.

Write down His promises and "*Be Ready*" to see them fulfilled. Post them in a place where you will see them daily and when the what-ifs threaten to drown you, cling to them. Find rest in His promises. I have 3×5 index cards taped to my prayer board, covered with His words. They are specific promises to me and/or my family and I lean into them heavily during times of fear, doubt, or uncertainty. Believe in them and breathe life into them. They will anchor your heart to where Jesus is taking you.

"*Be Ready*" for the people that He will bring to sit with you in the waiting room. People that were divinely placed there to help you get through it. Remember the story about my very special friend that reached out to me several times during my storm? God was placing my name on her heart and when I finally let my guard down and allowed her in, God used her to open doors to healing that were absolutely life-changing! "*Be Ready*" for these God-given people and situations to come into your life.

"*Be Ready*" for His goodness... It's coming! And don't forget the power of the rearview mirror. I often find it helpful to reflect on His goodness during previously weathered storms, no matter how painful the outcome, because I have always seen His love for me in the answers, sometimes even years later. When I reflect back on His goodness, it gives me peace in the waiting because I know He is faithful.

"*Be Ready*" for His provisions. Whatever His answer, and however it may differ from your expectations, be ready for His provisions. He will always provide everything you need.

"*Be Ready*." It's a concept that I love because it gives me something to *do,* an action that I can take, in the waiting. It anchors my heart in His peace, hope, and rest. And because I am keeping my focus on His faithfulness, His promises, and His goodness, it plants seeds of gratitude in my heart and I find myself so thankful for His presence in the middle of the storm. He is a good, good Father… and He loves you very much.

You see, over the last year, God has spoken to me regularly about trusting Him in the waiting room, trusting in His timing and His promises, even when I struggle to see anything moving or changing around me. But if I can hit the pause button again and share another story with you, I'll probably never forget the time that He interrupted my thoughts and connected His waiting room, and His spoken promises over my life, to my complete and utter impatience with two tiny little tree saplings in our yard. Let me explain…

About three years ago, my son and I planted two little 5" Blue Spruce tree saplings in our backyard. Our local Forest Service was giving them away for free, so we drove nearly 60 miles each way to pick up our saplings. We were eager and excited at the opportunity to plant Blue Spruce trees in our backyard. They are a prized tree here in Colorado, absolutely beautiful when fully grown, and very expensive to purchase, I might add. So, I certainly didn't mind the extra work involved in growing my own if it meant that I could be rewarded with such an amazing view out my living room window within a few years!

At pickup, the ranger suggested that we take two tree

saplings because he said only about 1 in 100 survive. Oh, but here's the thing… He didn't know me. I was determined to see these little beauties grow and thrive.

I'll save you the details and fast forward through the part of the story where we extensively researched their planting and care, picked the perfect spot, and carefully managed their growth and wellbeing over the next three years… to the part where I excitedly tell you that those little saplings are still doing exceptionally well today, all 8" of them!

Did you sense a bit of sarcasm there? Because it was layered pretty heavily on that last sentence. Three years… three years… and they stand a whopping 8" tall! And I find myself so frustrated.

You see, I had envisioned that, given the right focus, attention, care, and faith, I would have two glorious Blue Spruce trees growing beautifully in my backyard by now. Maybe only three to five feet tall or so, but a delightful and stunning reward for all my hard work and dedication. But as I look out my living room window, I can barely see the tops of them over the layer of protective rock that was carefully placed around them.

And one day, as I'm staring down at one of these little saplings in utter discontent, I begin to make important connections in my heart…

Do only 1 in 100 survive because of the time it takes between the *planting of the promise* and the *fruition of the beautiful view*?

Does the caretaker grow frustrated, like me, and give up, leaving the little saplings to whatever growth they make on their own, with no attention to their needs or nourishment?

And I'm sure you can see where I'm headed with this because it's right where God keeps taking me over and over in my life and in my calling:

Sometimes God plants seeds, in our heart, promises and visions for our future, and His words bring us hope and encouragement, but He is still asking us to sit in His waiting room and trust in His timing...

Maybe you are praying over a broken marriage.

Maybe you are praying for peace and joy in your own heart.

Maybe you are praying for a divine opportunity to open up in your career.

Maybe you are praying over a child that is struggling or a difficult decision that you need to make.

Or perhaps you are praying for a family member that is facing their own difficult season.

Whatever the situation, you are faithfully giving it over to Him. You are taking His seeds, His promises for your life and future, and you are planting them in your heart, watering them with prayer, and carefully tending to your thoughts and feelings so that you nourish them and they take root in your spirit.

And suddenly, you look down at your little saplings, your circumstances, your view, seemingly unchanged, and you're left wondering…

How long, God? How long? How long will you watch? How long will you wait? I'm tired. I'm weary. I'm hurting. I need you to come through for me, today.

Hear my heart on this, friends… I deeply understand.

I have many visions and promises written down on my prayer board; words that He has spoken to (or over) me about my life, my family, my circumstances, my calling, and/or my future. I have leaned in. I have faithfully nourished them, prayed over them, and taken care to guard them and steward them. And while I find His presence and His reassurance to be the most comforting and beautiful part of every day, sometimes I still find myself feeling tired and discouraged.

Sometimes I still catch myself looking over my neighbor's fence, my eyes fixed on her gorgeous 30' tall Blue Spruce trees, and wondering why I'm still standing over this 8" sapling. And here is what He continues to speak to my heart, even today:

Trusting Him, stepping out towards Him, and fully committing, also means trusting in His all-knowing and perfect timing for my life.

Trusting that whatever He is weaving together in the details, in the quiet, in the wait, is better than anything that I could have dreamed for myself; that the work He is doing in the unseen will produce a more beautiful fruit and future than I could ever imagine.

Trusting that the space He has made for my growth in the process waters the roots that stabilize me and draw my heart closer to His.

Trusting He is a good, good Father and He loves me too much to leave me here, staring at these 8" saplings, forever. That He will make good on His promises.

And, you see, all of that has me looped back to one of the things we shared very early on in the journey:

We are not expected to blindly trust or release control into the hands of a God that we don't know. He is calling us to draw close to Him and fall into a personal relationship with Him; to set our pain, our burdens, our fear and confusion, and even our anger at His feet, and let Him hold us.

He has been pouring over us all throughout this process. He has been redefining and reweaving our identity, pressing on us to see ourselves through His lenses. And all the while, He has been faithfully showing us who He is... the God who provides, the God who shows up, the God who stays, the God who heals, and the God who sees me, and know this, He sees you.

He sees our hearts. He sees our fears and our dreams. And His love for us is beyond our comprehension; beyond anything we can wrap our heads around;

beyond anything we can imagine. And in truly allowing all of that to take root in our hearts, we begin to understand He is a Father we can trust with His plan over our lives and we can trust in His timing as well.

I know waiting to see His promises realized can be hard. Sometimes, like David, it's so difficult to understand why He isn't reaching in and changing our circumstances today.

I know painful seasons can leave you struggling to breathe as you wait to see His plan unfold; that it can feel like some seeds are producing no fruit, regardless of how you take care to pray over them and give praise for them.

But I guarantee you this…

If God has given you His promise, then He will make good on it. He will be faithful.

Don't give up on your saplings. Keep seeking His heart. Draw close and be near to Him. Faithfully water what He has planted and "*Be Ready.*" Be ready to feel Him. Be ready for Him to fulfill every promise. Be ready for the people that He will bring into your life to sit with you and help you through it. Be ready for His goodness and His provisions. Focus on Him. He is the God who delivers. It may not always be the answer that we seek, and we may not always understand the wait, but He is always good and faithful and we are always safe in His hands.

...

"I waited and waited and waited some more, patiently, knowing God would come through for me. Then, at last, he bent down and listened to my cry.

He stooped down to lift me out of danger from the desolate pit I was in, out of the muddy mess I had fallen into.

Now he's lifted me up to a firm, secure place and steadied me while I walk along his ascending path. A new song for a new day rises up in me every time I think about how he breaks through for me!

Ecstatic praise pours out of my mouth until everyone hears how God has set me free. Many will see his miracles; they'll stand in awe of God and fall in love with him!

Blessing after blessing comes to those who love and trust the Lord..." (Psalm 40:1-4 TPT)

...

"We thank you, O God! We give thanks because you are near." (Psalm 75:1 NLT)

Chapter 24

The Joy Journey

I'd like to take a moment, a quick chapter, to just check in with your heart and recap some of the ground that we have covered so far on this journey. How are you doing, my friend? Truly.

If I may extend a note of encouragement...

It takes a tremendous amount of commitment and courage to walk through a healing process. Chasing joy is not always an easy, comfortable ride. In fact, it has probably been harder than you expected at times. I feel the same. But, I'm so incredibly grateful you are here. And I'm so very excited about the work that we are doing together.

Joy. What a beautiful promise. It is not defined by a season or an emotion. It's simply and beautifully a process of placing our hearts in God's loving hands; drawing close to Him so we may deeply know His heart; allowing that very real relationship to fully anchor our hope and peace to His promises; while wholly and completely accepting His truths about our identity and submitting our lives to His plan, His timing, His calling, and His loving protection.

Wow. That's powerful.

Joy is not a destination that we are racing towards. It's not a finish line we have to push harder, longer, and faster to reach so that we can win the grand prize, the glory, or His favor. No... Joy is something we can find right here, even in the middle of a storm or a difficult season.

Joy is in the healing.

Joy is in the deepening of our relationship with Jesus.

Joy is in discovering who we are in Him and how much He loves us.

Joy is knowing we are never alone.

Joy is knowing His grace is sufficient.

Joy is delighting in His touch, His voice, and His love.

Joy is resting in His promises.

And my friends, I'll say it again...

Joy is a beautiful gift of the journey and a piece of our Father's heart.

As we are nearing the end of our time here together, it can be easy to imagine some sort of false finish line that labels us as either a winner or a DNF (Did Not Finish), but don't get tangled up in those terms, or that mindset. Joy is found right here, in this moment, when we realize how truly, deeply, and unconditionally we are loved by Him and we allow that truth to pour into *every* aspect of our lives.

And as I allow that truth to sink in, I'm once again brought back to where it all started... with the bleeding woman in the crowd. Why? Because it all starts with drawing close to His heart and letting His healing touch move through us.

You see, if joy was a recipe, one of the main ingredients would be healing.

And the truth is, when it comes to my own personal healing, I don't know where I'd be without Jesus. He came to heal not only the physically lame, but also those with a crippled heart, and that's exactly where He found me. He is the One True Healer and He can heal you in ways you didn't think possible. And even better, He will bring people to sit with you and help you through it.

Trust me, *I'm still very much a work in progress*, but He faithfully meets me every day with grace and love. And like the perfect Father that He is, when I fall flat on my face (*as I so often do*), He picks me up, dusts me off, and reminds me I am His. He pours into me and gives me the strength, courage, and hope to face another day, another breath, another link, and another step. It's all about Jesus!

If I could reassure you of one thing on this journey, it would be this:

Do not anchor your faith, your healing, or your hope of what the future holds in what you can see, achieve, or understand, but rather, *what Jesus can do within you*. He loves you more than you know and He is always for you! He will make a way! And He *will* fill your cup again, until it overflows.

But what seems impossible to you is never impossible to God! (Matthew 19:26 TPT)

Are you feeling that deep in your soul? Are you feeling His gentle reassurance that He is there and He is guiding you? Lean into it. Believe in it. Believe in Him. His goodness and His faithfulness will never let you down.

In so many ways, it's true, this journey has been all about the incredible power of Jesus, for when He moves, I am completely overwhelmed by all that can be accomplished with the touch of His hands. But healing can be a lot of hard work too. And it's okay to admit that here, as well.

One step forward. Two steps backwards. Leaning in. Shaking in doubt. Then resolving yourself to lean in again. Tripping. Crumbling. Dusting off and standing back up. Purposeful work, but hard work nonetheless.

When God tells us that He's going to take us *through* the healing process instead of out of the painful situation, it's not always the answer we so desperately wanted. And sometimes the journey gets hard, just plain hard. There's no other way to describe it.

But remember this… You're never alone and you are never a disappointment. You are not failing or falling short when you shake in doubt, trip, or crumble on the bathroom floor. *You are healing and it's a process. Not a race to perfection, but a challenging and beautiful journey covered in His grace.*

In the year that followed my decision to chase joy, I found myself facing bucketloads of unresolved and unhealed issues; huge scars that had been painfully dug into my heart; threads of my life that were tightly woven around my spirit like a protective shield, assuring that no one would ever have the same access to my vulnerable, tender, and raw places again. And though I dedicated myself to speaking life into His promises, over and over, the decluttering process still greatly challenged me at times.

In the beginning, I fought His road to healing often. I would resist His gentle nudges to revisit my painful wounds, choosing instead to hold onto my protective walls and close the doors on His touch. I stalled often, coming to a complete stop in the middle of the road, arguing that the resurfaced pain and the idea of new vulnerability was more than my heart could manage. "I can't go there, God. Please don't ask me to. This all just hurts… too much."

And friends, He would sit with me there - every single

stumble, every doubt, every push back - without fail, listening to my fear and pain while gently and lovingly encouraging my heart to keep pushing through, all while reminding me that I was *safe* with Him. Safe, my friends. Safe. And that's a very big word when your heart has been shattered. *I was safe with Him.* And believe this, He will do the same for you.

You see, the journey to joy is never made without some painful realizations about our own hearts and maybe you have been feeling a bit of that too? Just remember this: We have a loving Heavenly Father who gently walks us through very deep heart transformations, always giving us grace where it so often feels undeserved, and we are reminded to give ourselves that same grace throughout the process. God is a loving God and He will slowly walk you through anything that challenges you on this journey, *without reprimand or shame.* Just take it to Him and lay it at His feet. He will see you through.

> *My child, don't underestimate the value of the discipline and training of the Lord God, or get depressed when he has to correct you. For the Lord's training of your life is the evidence of his faithful love. And when he draws you to himself, it proves you are his delightful child.* (Hebrews 12:5-6 TPT)

The truth is, sometimes Jesus will have to step in and gently guide you to move something unhealthy to the trash pile – judgment, unkind comments about others, unkind thoughts about yourself - but if you draw close to Him and lean into His healing, you will begin to feel an incredible transformation process taking place in your heart. Healing and joy will slowly begin to pour into even the darkest cracks and crevices. It may be a hardly noticeable stream at first, bounced about by rocks of doubt, shame, and insecurities, but it will water the seeds of hope that God has planted in you as you begin to feel Him working through you.

But also remember this... Chasing joy was never a checklist that you had to work down in order to be good enough to earn His outpouring of love. The truth is, He delighted in you long before you started this journey.

God didn't draw any closer to you or love you any more than He did before you started this process.

You are not somehow more worthy, more special, or more important to Him now than you were before. Don't believe the lie that the harder you work, the more of God's favor you will earn. He was always pouring it out over you. His love, His favor, is a beautiful gift, wrapped in grace and given freely to you, every day, as it always has been and always will be.

So, what exactly is the point of the links, the process, the joy journey itself?

Well, simply put, left unhealed and unresolved, that debris, that clutter that He's working through, often creates a barrier between what He is pouring out and our willingness to receive. You see, I found a pattern in my own life that, once realized, suddenly changed everything…

When Jesus would say, "I love you," my shame would answer, "you can't possibly."

When Jesus would say, "I am here," my perfectionism would answer, "I'm not good enough yet. Hold on… let me clean up a few things."

When Jesus would say, "I can heal that," my need for control would answer, "but, I can't give it to you."

When Jesus would say, "I have a calling on your life," my unhealed heart and fractured identity would respond, "You must mean someone else. I'm too broken."

You see, God was *always* speaking to me, loving on me, and pouring out over me, but I simply wasn't receptive to it because of the barriers that I had built between His voice and my heart. That's what this part of the journey came down to for me. Not a checklist to make myself worthy, but a process of removing the clutter so I could fully hear and receive His heart. The process of building a relationship with Him and drawing closer to Him so I could learn what He's been speaking all along.

And, I pray you are feeling that today. I pray you are feeling God as He moves through your broken seasons and the remnants and debris left behind. And as His healing touch pours through you, I pray you begin to

God was always speaking to me, loving me, and pouring out over me, but I simply wasn't receptive to it because of the barriers that I had built between His voice and my heart.

fully allow His truths and His voice to breathe life and joy back into your bruised and broken heart.

Believe me, I know how sometimes just taking that next step, or that next breath, feels like it challenges our spirits more than we can handle. And I know how we can struggle to find our footing again after a really big fall. But, please hear my heart on this very important and encouraging truth...

The hard work that you are doing now... it matters!

The truth is, you are doing a lot more than walking through a season of healing and chasing joy. You, my friend, are breaking multi-generational chains. You are standing in the gap for your family. You are choosing to face the hard, heal old wounds, and stare down the enemy and guess what ...

Your children are watching. Your friends are watching. Your family is watching. And you are fighting battles not just in the natural realm, but in the spiritual as well. And it's shaking things up, not only within you, but all around you.

As you journey through healing, chasing Jesus and joy, your light and your testimony are becoming a bright beacon of hope for all those who know you.

You see, all that *difficult*, all that *challenging*, all that *painful* stuff in the journey, while we may find that it momentarily discourages us and fuels thoughts and feelings of utter defeat, we must always (*always*) remember this…

Our journey… it matters.

Our hard work… it matters.

Our healing… it matters.

Why? Because…

Our hearts matter to Him *and*…

As we rise, Jesus will use our healing to bring others with us.

Whew… let's just sit on that last powerful note for one more moment…

As you rise, my friend, Jesus will use your healing to bring others with you.

No matter how we stumble. No matter how we struggle. No matter how we fall or find ourselves discouraged, He will use our journey, our hearts, and our willingness to push through, to reach out and pull others out of the darkness and into the light of His hope, His love, and His joy today! He will use our story of His grace and His presence in the hard, in the wilderness, to remind others that we don't ever have to earn His love. No, we are simply and beautifully called to lean into it and allow it to pour through us and heal us; to lean into Him and let Him guide us through.

And hear this…

Through your journey, my friend, you are giving your children the beautiful gift of a new floor. Your ceiling - *your healing, your joy, the place to which you rise* - becomes your child's very foundation that they will spend the rest of their lives building upon; *the place from which they will begin the journey themselves.*

You see, I know firsthand how some days can be so difficult. I know that faith isn't always easy to lean into, especially when we don't see a path leading us from where we are standing to where He is promising to take us. And I know how sometimes it can feel like the fear is mounting, the obstacles are growing, and the only thing we have the strength to do is speak His truths over our journey and allow Him to carry the rest. And that's ok. He is there. And He is good. He *will* reach into the rubble and He *will* carry you out.

But I also know that, one last time, joy does not come passively. We have to be mindful of what we allow to pour through our thoughts and hearts, what we are choosing to water and allow to root in our spirits, because although the journey is not always easy, He promises *it will always be worth it.*

Draw close. Know Him. And the rest of it, you will figure out on the journey… *together.*

So, if you can feel the change stirring deep in your soul; if you feel God healing the pieces of you that were buried so deep that they were all but forgotten; if you feel warmth, hope and joy returning and you slowly sense the walls around your heart beginning to crumble, then allow this simple truth to encourage you today....

God is moving in ways you never imagined. You do not just *feel* different. You *are* different. He is transforming you. Thank Him for it. Water it. And delight in it. Let it feed your heart and your spirit, today.

And if you are struggling to feel change, if you feel painfully weighed down, heavy, or defeated, I just invite you to continue to take that to Him, over and over, and let Him continue to pour through it. Let Him heal you, link by link, as He loves on you and reminds you how incredibly special you are to Him.

I know one thing for certain, He is the God who sees, the God who stays, the God who heals, and *the God who makes the impossible possible.* And you mean so much to Him. Don't give up. Don't turn back. Your hard work matters more than you know. Just keep bringing your heart to him and letting Him move through it. Push through the hard together and let Him show you the way.

I am always praying for your journey. I am standing with you in faith and confidence that He will deliver. Keep your eyes on Him. You will not fail. Keep seeking His heart and letting Him meet you wherever you are. And hold tight to the words that He has spoken over your life, because He *is* the God who comes through on His promises. And He will come through for you.

Chapter 25

There's Power in Your Story

Your story, yes yours, has a *tremendous* amount of healing power.

Remember how we discussed in the previous chapter that God will use you (and your journey) to lift others? How you (*yes, you!*) will become a beacon of hope? Well, in this chapter we are going to dive a bit deeper into that very powerful truth and allow it to become a planted seed in our hearts. Believe it, today! As you rise, He will use you, and your story, to help others.

…

Sometimes the greatest gift we can receive in the wilderness is the outstretched hand of someone who has been there. Someone with a story of hope. Someone with a story of overcoming. Someone with a story that says your journey doesn't end here. This isn't your last chapter.

The truth is, if you feel like you are in a difficult season and trudging through the hard right now, your story has the power to make someone feel less alone; to give someone the strength to take that next step towards healing; to encourage and lift someone on even the grayest days because they feel seen and understood.

Your story, yes yours, has the tremendous power today to minister to someone's heart.

You see, God will use our imperfect (and even messy) journey to reach someone that He divinely places in our path. Someone that so desperately seeks to be seen and touched in those broken and shattered places deep inside their heart. Someone who, right now, likely feels lost and alone. I've been there and I have felt that. And I'm betting you have too.

And while I know that sharing our story is hard, that it can make us feel very vulnerable because we have been trained by society to self-preserve by saving face, *I also know that when we lift the veil of perfection, we create space for those around us to be imperfect and share in their brokenness as well.* And that's a truly powerful thing!

When we can share our broken places and shattered pieces with each other, we can pray for each other, lift each other, stand in the gap for each other, and share God's love with each other.

Sharing your story doesn't mean you have to build a blog or write a book, although if you feel led, I'll be your first fan and biggest cheerleader! Most of the time, though, sharing your story simply means that you ask God to use your journey to help someone that He divinely places in your path and then you open your heart to that nudge, His gentle push, and you press in.

You see, someone needs to know that they are not alone. Someone needs to know that there is hope.

Someone needs to know that there is a brighter tomorrow.

Someone needs to know that their story doesn't end here; that He is with them right now, holding them close, making a way through the wilderness, and bringing them to a place of peace.

Someone needs to know that He can heal their most broken pieces and He has already written their next chapter… and it's beautiful.

Someone needs to know that they *never* have to fit a man-made mold or definition of *enough* of anything; that they never have to "*earn*" the complete, beautiful, and perfect outpouring of His love and grace.

Someone needs to know that He will meet them right where they are, without reservation or shame, no matter what road they have traveled and what choices they have made, and He will love them into their healing.

And friends, it doesn't matter if you think you are too loud, too introverted, too blunt, too grammatically incorrect, too poor of a public speaker (so did Moses!), too simple, too country, too (*insert whatever holds you back*) …

…because here's the key:

He will be with you.

He will guide your steps and your words, and you will be the perfect fit for the person that He places in your path.

Someone will hear your message because of exactly who you are and the One who walks with you.

You see, I will never be everyone's cup of tea, but maybe that person that I don't reach finds a kindred link to you. That's what's so beautiful about our individuality and uniqueness… because God designs us with diversity in personality so that we may share His love in our own ways and reach our own tribes, our own community of kindred spirits, for Him.

So, if you have walked through the wilderness and felt His touch, His love, and His healing power flow through your circumstances, if it has given you strength, hope, rest, and even joy in the difficult seasons, allow Him to use your hard to help another.

Live with a heart that seeks to help those that He divinely places in your path. Live to share His heart with the hurting.

There's just one question left to ask…

What's holding you back?

Tell you what… I'll go first:

When God Calls Me Out of My Safe Space

One Halloween when I was in my early twenties and dating my (*now*) husband, he thought it would be a fun idea to take me to a local haunted house. Now, I am definitely your play-it-safe girl. I am almost guaranteed to be painfully and boringly risk-averse in many thrill-seeking, life-on-the-edge type situations, and that *does* include haunted houses in my book.

But on this day, I was like an out-of-control bobble head, the rise and fall of my face signaling *yes*, while all my insides were quite literally screaming, *Lord, no!* And just like that, as if someone had completely taken over my last bit of common sense, I agreed to walk through a terrifying maze of heart-stopping horror with this really cute boy, all because… I really liked him.

How did I get here?

But worry not because this very cute and amazing guy absolutely *promised* me that he would be with me every step of the way and I would never be alone.

Well, as I'm sure you have already guessed, about midway through the haunted house, we got separated (at least that's how he tells the story). Now, picture it…

There I stood, my fight or flight had up and left the building; I was in full-blown freeze mode. Squeezing my eyes as tightly closed as possible, I tried to simply *will* it all away. Completely immobilized by fear, I ultimately convinced myself that staying frozen in this

spot all night was far better than the alternative...
Opening my eyes and taking the next step forward.

Yes, I was *that* girl, the kind that you definitely don't take into a haunted house. The kind you only hope to have available in a zombie apocalypse so you can leave her behind as an easy distraction, an easy meal.

As I reflect back more seriously on that memory, that story we so often laugh about now, I see a painful pattern emerge, evidence of a life lived fearfully in the safe-zone. I realize just how many times I have found myself in that same frozen state, unable to move forward because I so greatly feared the unknowns...

Social situations.

Family situations.

Career opportunities.

Adventure opportunities.

And even God-given calling opportunities.

All moving past me, just waiting for me to reach out and grab them, to live life fully alive, as I stood completely immobile, frozen in place, simply too afraid to jump.

And in that deep reflection, I begin to understand that I have not only *welcomed* this approach to life, but I have fully embraced it. Why? Because I have erroneously convinced myself that if I remain in my safe-space,

265

never taking a road that leads into the unfamiliar, then I will be able to maintain control over all the outcomes.

I can control what touches and affects my heart. I can control my disappointments and my failures. I can control my fear of the unknown (by simply not venturing into it). And I can control what people think of me… yes, that too.

Of course, we know in our hearts that believing in this kind of power or influence is undoubtedly deeply flawed thinking, but we still chase that sense of control because we fear the crushing damage that could, and would, occur if we truly let go.

If this speaks to you, I'm right there with you. It can be both painful and terrifying to jump when you've spent your entire life protecting your heart. Just the thought of stepping out can make your legs feel weak and your stomach drop. And like me, you may find yourself frozen in place, desperately seeking the comfort and protection of your familiar safe-zone often.

But I'm growing, my friends! I'm healing! And my stay-safe approach is being beautifully challenged.

You see, God often calls us to jump *with* Him into our purpose, our calling, and to rest in the fact that He is already there, even in the uncomfortable and the unknown. He has already written the next chapter and all we have to do is trust Him; all we have to do is open our eyes, open our hearts, and take that next step *with* Him.

The invitation is there and it's completely up to me to decide...

Follow Him and fully fall into Him, live life fully alive, or allow my fear to hold me back and remain frozen in my "safe" space indefinitely?

Make no mistake - He will wait for me (and you) - but I know that the fulfillment of my freedom and His promise of joy is on the other side and I know that all I have to do is collect my courage and jump... fully into His arms.

God is so incredibly good and I know that any plan He has in store for you is absolutely beautiful and full of blessings. He *is* life. His plan *becomes* the cup that overflows. He guides you to a place of joy, peace, and rest. And in His presence and His calling, you are truly safe. And now we just have to make the decision to trust and follow, even if we are afraid.

Here's the best part, though...

Unlike my (*amazing and forgiven*) husband who totally dropped the ball that night at the haunted house, God will never (*ever, ever!*) leave you to walk through anything alone. Whatever He is calling you to journey through, He will be right by your side.

When you feel fear, you can whisper to Him that you are afraid. When you feel frozen in place, you can call His name. When your eyes are squeezed shut and you're terrified to take that next step, to see what's around the next corner, you can trust Him to hold you through it. And when you feel ill-equipped to make it through whatever you are facing, you can ask Him to remind you who you are and Whose you are.

He will always speak life into your heart, filling you with His truths, His presence, and His guidance throughout the journey.

Full Circle

So, let's bring this full circle…

Your story, yes yours, has a *tremendous* amount of healing power. You can use your journey, your testimony, your hard, to reach out and grab the hands of others and bring them up with you.

God may divinely place someone in your path that needs your message of hope. And if He does, you will be the precise fit and perfectly equipped. But it may mean that you have to drop the veil and trust Him *in the vulnerable*; it may truly call you out of your safe space and thrust you into the unknown. I know it has for me… a few times over.

But there have been so many blessings in simply following His calling. Your cup will overflow as He uses you to touch the lives of others. Trust me! His power will flow through your heart and you will feel joy in His presence as you step into His plan and follow His lead.

But I won't leave you there. I'm going to share with you some additional encouragement because I know how those moments just before we step into that divinely-placed circumstance can truly challenge our hearts. I know how we can be shaking our head *yes* and fighting to drown our mind's panicking screams of *no!* It's okay, you'll hear no shame from me. Fear is very real. But so are His truths.

So, when you find yourself afraid of whatever God is calling you to do, I pray that these verses give you the strength and courage to fully jump in...

You are able because He has already equipped you.

For we are God's masterpiece. He has created us anew in Christ Jesus, so we can do the good things he planned for us long ago. (Ephesians 2:10 NLT)

You will never walk alone because He is already there.

Do not be afraid or discouraged, for the LORD will personally go ahead of you. He will be with you; he will neither fail you nor abandon you. (Deuteronomy 31:8 NLT)

You are safe in His hands because He will always protect you and provide for you.

The LORD says, "I will guide you along the best pathway for your life. I will advise you and watch over you." (Psalm 32:8 NLT)

You don't need a road map that tells you how you will get there because He will show you the way.

Trust in the LORD with all your heart; do not depend on your own understanding. Seek his will in all you do, and he will show you which path to take.
(Proverbs 3:5-6 NLT)

You don't have to fear the outcome because He is so faithful and good. His plans for your life will bless you beyond anything you can comprehend.

"For I know the plans I have for you," says the LORD. "They are plans for good and not for disaster, to give you a future and a hope. (Jeremiah 29:11 NLT)

Whatever divine situation that He places in our path, wherever He calls us to travel, all we have to do is choose to fully fall into Him. We can trust Him, even in the unfamiliar, vulnerable, and uncomfortable, because we know that He will *always* show up. And when we are afraid, we can rest in the truth that He will always be faithful; that as we lean into Him, He will pour His strength and His guidance into us for the journey ahead.

For I can do everything through Christ, who gives me strength. (Philippians 4:13 NLT)

And here's the beautiful and life-giving lesson that I learned along the way…

If we want to jump into His calling for our lives, His path for our future, then we have to accept His invitation to *step out of the boat*. It *will* mean fully embracing the unknowns simply and beautifully because of one powerful truth:

Who we know is so much more important than *what* we know.

It does not mean that there will always be an absence of fear. It simply and gloriously means that we trust and choose the One who calls us more.

We can do this. We can fall into His plan, His calling, and His arms. Take my hand. Step out with me. And let's watch Him absolutely shake our comfort zones and *use our story and our willingness to share it* in the most beautiful and powerful ways!!

Chapter 26

Be The Rare

Fun fact: Did you know that in the medical field, the term "zebra" is often used to describe a rare, surprising, or exotic diagnosis. The association is said to have originated from the idea that it is much more common to encounter a horse, but a zebra is quite rare indeed.

Lately, I feel like my Heavenly Father has been placing a gentle and relevant reminder on my heart...

The truth is, pain and unhealed wounds often cause us to focus strictly inward and, as a result, we have lost our warmth and become disconnected. Many times, we don't even notice the pain around us because the pain within us is so all-consuming.

Then there's the added layer that when we travel through a difficult season, we frequently erect strong impenetrable walls in order to protect our already bruised and broken hearts. We eventually learn to operate in survival mode and we all-too-soon begin to face life with our heads down. It's an isolating and difficult road, but preferred over the perceived only possible other alternative, further damage.

I think one of the things that shocked me most when I became a mother was when someone told me that the only way to make my son strong enough to endure this world was to expose him to the cruelty of it early on and allow it to toughen him up. "*Trust me*," they said, "*he will figure out how to grow a thicker skin and survive. We all do.*" And something about that just didn't sit right with me. I couldn't figure out why giving lessons on how to build walls around his precious little heart was listed on page two of the parenting instruction manual.

But that's often how we function, isn't it? In protection and survival mode, with our heads down and our focus inward. Did you know that *toughen up* is often likened to *becoming more stoic?* And stoicism is defined as, *the endurance of pain or hardship without the display of feelings and without complaint.** Ouch. And soon enough, we find ourselves growing cold, distant, unemotional, indifferent, and apathetic, even. All because we are trying our best to just survive.

But is that really how we've been designed to operate? Disconnected. Protecting. It all just hurts my heart, deeply.

And here's the powerful and beautiful miracle and message that God has been pouring into me lately in my own journey...

Just as I do not want my child to believe that happiness requires a thick skin, high walls, and a survival-based approach to life, my Heavenly Father's heart also aches when He sees me living this way. But you see, there is a cure for this conditioned response; there is another way.

My friends, something truly remarkable happens when God starts healing you. Something shifts when you walk through this journey of chasing joy in even the most difficult seasons. Because when all that debris is redefined and His love pours through you and all of your pain, your heart begins to completely transform. You no longer need walls of anger and resentment for protection. You no longer live in fear that if given the chance, the enemy may deliver one final blow that you simply cannot survive. And you no longer hide your true self away from the world, drowning in insecurities, shame, and doubt. No...

When your heart becomes deeply (*deeply*) anchored in the truth that you are the daughter of a King and you are chosen, wanted, loved, and have an irreplaceable role and purpose, your unwavering faith in His truths about your identity suddenly begins to negate your survival-based fight-or-flight conditioned response and former way of life!

And as we near the end of this book, I am deeply hoping that this journey has brought you closer to that very place.

Because the truth is, "toughen up" is in the world's guidebook, not God's.

You see, we don't have to be cold and distant to survive. We don't have to hide in shame or function out of fear-based self-preservation. We don't even have to keep our heads down and our focus inward to avoid further damage. We just have to draw closer to Him and as He pours His goodness into our hearts...

We rise and rest in the identity that He places in us.

The truth is, the world and the enemy *do not* have the power to penetrate our identity in Him or shake our foundation. We are *solidly* anchored.

And here's the miracle in the message...

When we have absolute faith in that truth, we will stop frantically protecting ourselves and something else will beautifully begin to pour out of us... His love.

So, while this chapter is short and simple and nothing extraordinarily mind-blowing, it is a beautiful and powerful challenge to touch on in our own personal journey. And here it is, my friends...

As your healing and your path to chasing joy in the hard solidly anchors you to God's truths about your identity, *use that change to propel you into action in another area of your life...*

Be the person that surprises them! Be the zebra! Be the rare!

Don't approach the broken world around you with your protective walls up and your head down...

Be the person that looks up, today.

Be the person that genuinely compliments.

Be the person that smiles.

Be the person that shows God's love in *completely unexpected* places.

Be the person that seeks opportunities to be used.

Be the person that forgives.

Be the person that gives grace.

Be the person that stops and notices, the good and the pain.

Be the person that sends the text.

Be the person that makes the call.

Be the person that truly cares.

Be the person that *sees the brokenness, and not just the symptoms.*

Be the person that touches their hearts.

Be the example of His love and grace.

Be... the rare, today.

When we rise and rest in the identity that He places in us, we will stop frantically protecting ourselves and something else will begin to beautifully pour out of us... His love.

And when you actively try to "*be the rare,*" something beautiful will begin to happen in your own life – you will become a lighthouse for those that are tired from being beaten against the rocks and are longing for healing as well. They will see His light in you and they will want to seek His healing and His joy too.

And if I share His love with my small piece of the world and you share His love with yours, maybe we can be a part of something so much bigger. Maybe we can be a witness to some truly incredible miracles as God moves.

So, which are you operating from today? Fear-based self-preservation or *the rare*?

You'll get no judgment from me. There are some hurts that just seal the heart's doors without so much as a warning. Our mind reasons that if we can just protect it, we may be able to find a way to survive.

But the truth is, we cannot accept His fulfillment of joy in our hearts if we are solely operating in survival mode because He is calling us into a life of *so much more*.

And like we discussed in chapter twenty-five, as we share His love and open our hearts with others, our testimony and our healing will be the message that touches the dark crevices of pain and brokenness all around us. And we will receive more and more joy as we feel Jesus move in this very special space.

Hear the invitation, today, and take the challenge, my friend. Be transformed. Be different. Be the rare.

Your lives light up the world. For how can you hide a city that stands on a hilltop? And who would light a lamp and then hide it in an obscure place? Instead, it's placed where everyone in the house can benefit from its light. So don't hide your light! Let it shine brightly before others, so that your commendable works will shine as light upon them, and then they will give their praise to your Father in heaven.

(Matthew 5:14-16 TPT)

* Oxford University Press (2021) wake. In: Lexico.com, Available at: https://www.lexico.com/definition/stoicism [Accessed 18/02/2022].

Chapter 27

Into His Healing

Jesus, please breathe new life into me. Speak your calling into my heart and light my path so that I may always follow where you lead. Thank you for your blessings. Thank you for your healing. And most of all, thank you for loving on me so much throughout this journey.

…

Fall into Me.

Let Go.

Hear My voice.

Allow My truths to break through your walls.

Allow My love to clear the debris, the fallout, and the damaging shards that continue to cause you pain.

Allow My touch to heal you, and…

Allow My heart to make you whole, again.

Step out of the boat.

Walk towards Me.

Trust Me.

Take My hand.

I am here. I am with you. And I will not let you drown.

And when you're ready… we will run…

Towards joy…

…and living fully alive…

Together!!

…

Those are His promises.

This is His heart, today.

And He will meet you right where you are.

…

My friends, the book is coming to an end, *but not the journey,* and I wanted to encourage you as you continue to walk forward into His healing…

What does it mean to have lasting, full, and deeply rooted joy, peace, and hope? Joy that isn't tied to the circumstances we face; Hope that isn't shaken or uprooted by the storms we weather; Faith that isn't deconstructed by a rocky season or an unexpected closed door. Because that is what God wants to give you, today. That is what it means to live fully alive! And while I'm 100% on the journey with you, still healing and growing, and I don't have all of the answers that I know your heart (and mine) are so desperately seeking, I *do* know the One who holds us right now and He has reminded me of so many things along the way.

My friend, you are not a product of your difficult seasons or defined by your mistakes, forever stuck in this cycle of pain, shame, and insecurity. *You are made new in Him.* He has called you His and He has promised to reweave your broken heart, to heal you, and to give you peace and hope. He can rewrite the labels that weigh you down, the brands that the enemy tries to forever place on your heart, and He can replace them with His truths…

You are chosen, seen, belonging, known, beautiful, gifted, special, irreplaceable, highly valuable, the light of the world, royal, holy, called, and with purpose. You are accepted, redeemed, forgiven, loved, and always enough. And He delights in you. Today.

I have hard days on the journey. Sometimes they are rough on many fronts. Sometimes my old scars, my old wounds, start calling my name and I begin to feel overwhelmed by life or my feelings. Those are the kind of days that threaten to shake my core into a spiral, a free-fall really. In the past, I would find myself questioning everything… His promises, His presence, His seeing me. That train of thought would quickly lead to another sort of doubt… My value and my calling. My very purpose. Then shame would come knocking. Or maybe sadness and hopelessness. *Or all of the above.*

Over time, I began to liken it to falling off the monkey bars in elementary school. The wind would get completely knocked out of me and even though it would take me less than a minute to find my breath again, those 10-15 seconds were filled with utter panic, fear, and doubt, quickly followed by shame and embarrassment, and I often just wanted to find a place to hide from the world. To hide from it all.

But that is also where His promises so beautifully and perfectly come into play, right? Because when we fall hard on the journey ahead, and we struggle to find our next breath, we know that we serve a Heavenly Father that loves us deeply and will ALWAYS breathe life back into us!

I cannot tell you the number of times that my heart has bounced up and down during the healing process. From moments of great breakthroughs to moments that were very difficult and painfully confusing. From moments where I thought that I had conquered a giant once and for all to moments where I realized that I picked it right back up… again. But if you find yourself struggling, can I just pause for a moment and reassure your heart…

He will cover you with his feathers. He will shelter you with his wings. His faithful promises are your armor and protection. (Psalm 91:4 NLT)

I faced days on the journey where the only hope that remained in me rested entirely on His promises; days when the storms would hit hard and I grew weak and tired. But the beautiful truth is that no matter the storm I faced, no matter the size of the waves, His promises, they always held. *He always held me.* His presence never wavered, no matter how hopeless, angry, confused, and frustrated I became.

You see, if we choose to solidly anchor our hearts to Him, there is just so much power in His words. Why?

(Because...) *Not one promise from God is empty of power. Nothing is impossible with God!*

(Luke 1:37 TPT)

How do I know? *Because I know Him.*

We may still fall off the monkey bars from time to time. We may still find ourselves completely breathless by the impact. But when we cling to Him, He will hold us close and His presence will calm the panic, the fear, and the doubt that is threatening our very peace and progress.

He will move through our pain and our heartbreak to heal us and breathe life back into us. And all we have to do is fall into Him. Trust Him with our journey and trust Him with our life. And once again, it all begins back where we first started, with the bleeding woman, because it all begins with drawing close and *knowing* Him. *Deeply knowing Him.*

It's never been about willing ourselves to submit or faking it until we make it. It's about our *relationship* with Him. It's about His love. It's about truly knowing His heart, because in seeking Him, we have grown to truly know Him. In drawing close, in feeling His presence pour over us, we have found that the surrender *and the faith* have become a natural extension of that very beautiful connection, of a life walked *with* Him.

Which so perfectly loops my heart right back to the story of Peter...

"Lord, if it's you..."

You see, when the disciples first saw Jesus on the water that day, they thought He was a ghost and they were terrified, crying out in fear. But then Jesus spoke reassurance, encouraging them not to be afraid. Why?

Because they knew exactly who He was.

And friends, hasn't He spoken those same words so many times in the middle of our storm? In the middle of this journey?

Don't be afraid, Shannon. Trust me.

You know who I am.

In Hebrews, chapter 13, verse 5, God shares His true heart with us: (My child,) "*I will never fail you.*" (NLT) And that's His unwavering promise still today. In fact, I love The Passion Translation's version of this verse because it so beautifully reads...

He promised you, "I will never leave you, never! And I will not loosen my grip on your life."

"I will not loosen my grip on your life."

And yet here are these disciples who, just hours before, had literally watched Jesus heal the sick and feed over five thousand men, plus women and children, from five loaves of bread and two fish! And even more amazing, Jesus had not simply supplied *enough*... no. His provisions were *in abundance*, as they always are. In fact, there were twelve baskets of leftover food collected!

Jesus had provided.

Jesus had healed.

Jesus had made the impossible *possible*.

And yet, only one disciple spoke up... Peter.

Sometimes I wonder if the rest of the disciples stood completely frozen in that boat. Sometimes I wonder if, even though they knew exactly who Jesus was, they still found themselves doubting His faithfulness when it came to their own lives, their own storms. *And if I'm honest, I can relate. I have been there too.*

Still afraid to trust. Still fearful that the next shoe would drop, the next wave would hit, and somehow God wouldn't be there. Afraid that this same Jesus that I had witnessed make the impossible possible over and over again, will simply not show up for me, not this time.

Now, I want to focus for just a minute on Peter's response…

"Lord, if it's you," Peter replied, "tell me to come to you on the water." (Matthew 14:28 NIV)

"Lord, if it's you…"

The truth is, sometimes, we just need a little reminder. A moment to focus on *Who* we are walking towards; *Who* it is that we are trusting; *Whose* arms are we falling into when we decide to let go.

Because remember…

Who we know is so much more important than *what* we know.

"Lord, if it's you…"

And the next part is key…

Then I will place my trust in you.

Why? … *because I know you.*

Because you are a good and faithful Father.

The truth is, we can have faith that in His hands the unbelievable becomes believable. We may even witness his divine power move in completely indescribable ways. And yet, we can still find ourselves absolutely terrified to walk out on that water.

But, here's the ultimate game changer, the detail in the clutter that allows our hearts to release control and truly begin to lean in and step out....

It is in that *deep and intimate relationship with Him, knowing Him and knowing His heart,* that we begin to find the courage and confidence to start the process of letting go and surrendering it *all* to Him.

Draw close. Come just as you are. And what we will beautifully grow to understand is that in focusing on that genuine relationship, that deep connection between His heart and ours, we will naturally begin to trust His touch, His provisions, and His guidance in *all* aspects of our lives.

My friends, it is in knowing Him, truly knowing Him, that we begin to understand that our lives placed in His hands are far better than any plans placed in our control.

And then, my friends, like Peter, we will call out...

"Lord, if it's you..."

I will trust you today...

I will trust you with this heartache.

I will trust you with this diagnosis.

I will trust you with this decision.

I will trust you with this season.

I will trust you with these finances.

I will trust you with this broken relationship.

I will trust you with my future, my next chapter, the outcome of this situation.

I will trust you with my heart.

I will trust you with my life.

You see, there's no shame in this message. There's no underlying expectation that we conquer our giant of fear with one swift blow. In fact, I'll admit right here that there were many times in my journey that I almost lost my grip on His promises as the rising panic threatened to drown me. It's completely normal. And if I might add, the enemy will absolutely use that time to begin to whisper lies as well; lies of defeat, unworthiness, or falling short.

And the truth is that sometimes when we are trusting Jesus, fully pressing in, and *our storm* is still roaring around us, we *may* momentarily lose focus. We *may* frantically look up, begin to evaluate our safety and our circumstances, and quickly start to question…

God, where are you? I'm trusting you, I'm leaning in. Why is the storm still raging around me? Why is the storm still raging inside me? Jesus, I'm so scared! Why have you abandoned me?

And it is in those moments of panic, those waves that threaten to sink you one final time, that I invite you to do one action, one pause, one thing that can make all the difference in your heart and in your spirit...

Silence everything else and listen for His voice. Listen for His heart. Listen for Him ...

... and you'll hear Him say...

"My child, you *know* me. You know *who* I am. Keep your eyes on me. I will protect you. I love you. These are my promises. And I will be faithful. I will not let you drown."

Because the truth is, each and every time that the panic overtook me and I lost my grip on His promises, He lovingly reminded me that *He will never lose His grip on me.*

"I will never leave you, never! And I will not loosen my grip on your life." (Hebrews 13:5 TPT)

Which loops me right back to Peter...

Because about that Peter, well he took several steps out of that boat. He was walking on water! For just a moment, he placed every fear, every what-if, every doubt in His Father's hands. He stepped out towards Jesus, fully embracing a moment of total faith and trust in God. But then, like we so often do, he looked around at the wind and waves, he looked around at his storm, and my friends, he became frightened and he began to sink.

And guess what the next verse says...

"Immediately, Jesus reached out his hand and caught him." (Matthew 14:31 NIV)

Immediately.

Jesus caught him. Scooped him right up. Protected him and loved him *no less.*

And He will catch you too. As many times as it takes.

Because He is a good and faithful Father and we are absolutely covered in His grace.

We are on a journey. Sometimes we will walk through the hard and feel very confused and sometimes we will dance in the sun and delight in the beauty. But He is a faithful Father and He is bringing us to a place of peace, hope and joy. He is the God who delivers. And He will deliver for you.

Don't look at the wilderness around you or the storm within you and think that you are lost or forgotten.

Don't give up hope and decide that a life lived here, in the uncomfortable but familiar pain, is easier than the next step forward.

Don't plant roots in the wilderness when He is calling you into a joy-filled life ahead.

Just keep pressing in. Keep taking it back to Him. Keep pushing forward... even if it's one tiny baby step at a time. Seek Him. Because, my friend...

It is all about the incredible healing power of Jesus!

To put my own transformation into words, a little over a year ago, when He took me by the hand in the middle of a dark and difficult season and encouraged me to lean into Him, this miraculous healing seemed as far away as one could possibly feel from a dream…

…But Jesus!

And that is exactly why I share my story and my personal journey with you. That is why this book is in your hands. Because if you find yourself in need of healing today, be it physical, emotional, or spiritual, I can promise you as someone who has been in a dark and difficult season with no hope in sight, that there is *more* than hope… there's a promise!

There is endless love and healing power available to you. There is joy. There is a new tomorrow. There is a cup that overflows! And His name is Jesus!

One day you'll look down and find yourself walking on water without understanding!

One day, you'll find the incredible joy we have been so deeply discussing in this book will take root and begin to grow and blossom in your heart!

One day, your feet will lift off the ground and you will begin to dance!

All because of Jesus!

You see, He is the ultimate paradigm shift creator. The God of absolutely incredible miracles. And best of all, He is 100% for you!

So, when the journey ahead gets hard and you struggle to understand, when you look around at your storm and you find yourself sinking, I just encourage you to pause and remember His truths.

Who is He? He is the One True Healer. Of the Body. Of the Heart. And of the Soul.

We need only to draw close to Him. To be near Him. To curl up at His feet or on His lap. And He will do the rest.

How do I know? *Because I know Him.*

And when He pours into you; when He deeply heals you; when He moves through your every pain and sorrow and fills your heart with joy and strength…

On that day when you look down and find yourself walking on water and His name is the most powerful and beautiful praise on your lips…

My sweet friend, remember this…

He is calling you to dance!

Dance in His freedom!

Dance in His joy!

Dance in His healing, hope, and peace!

Dance in His presence!

Dance in His goodness!

Just Dance!

Are you ready? I'm ready!

Let's move beyond our safe space and fall fully into His arms! Let's invite Him to be our beginning and our end and watch Him take our impossible and make it possible! Let's embrace what it means to live fully alive in Jesus today!

Let's find joy… *together*… and shake the Kingdom for Him!!

I'm so incredibly excited for you! Blessings on your journey ahead! May you feel Him pour over you today and every day!

…

Eight Truths About God's Love To Carry With You

Before we part, I just wanted to encourage you to read through these eight truths and allow them to deeply take root in your heart today! Make these declarations over your life, and your journey ahead, and allow them to bring you hope, encouragement, and strength.

I am deeply loved by a Heavenly Father that knows me by name.

He delights in me today, right now, in this very moment, just as I am. Even in the moments when I fall short or fail, He picks me up, dusts me off, and proudly calls me His. I do not have to earn His love, chase perfection, or be "enough." I am simply, beautifully, and unconditionally His child... because He chose me. Because He sees me. And because He loves me that much.

My pain, my struggles, my difficult seasons...
they do not go unnoticed or disregarded.

My "little" is never insignificant to Him and I am never left to make the journey alone. Although sometimes I find myself sitting in His waiting room, desperately clinging to His promises for a brighter tomorrow, I know that He is a good and faithful Father and He will always see me through. He will reweave my pain to create something beautiful for my future.

The invitation will always read, "Come Just As
You Are."

He will meet me there... in my pain. In my anger. In my doubt and confusion. In my brokenness. There is no need to clean up the mess. He will never ask me to look my best before I approach Him with my worst. He wants me today, just as I am, and He will hold me. Weep with me. Dream for me. And encourage my heart.

He is the God of hope.

When I stand staring at my circumstance, my storms threatening to overtake me at any moment, I can always seek peace in His presence and His promises. I have a Heavenly Father that will always (always) make a way. When the sheets of rain leave me frozen in fear or pain and I cannot see a path through the storm, I can trust Him to calm the seas, part the waters, and guide me through. This is not the end of my story.

He is always working in the details, often in the unseen, bringing me ever-closer to a place of peace, hope, and even joy.

When a door closes, I will seek His guidance. When I see a love note from Him, I will thank Him for pouring over my heart. When my circumstances shift and opportunity knocks, I will give thanks for His blessings. My life is not a series of coincidences. It's a series of changes that take place when I choose to lean into Him and I begin to recognize His love, His goodness, and His favor all around me.

I am called to something bigger... and I'm ready!

He has placed gifts inside of me and a calling on my heart. He calls me beautiful and chosen. His calling for my life will be kingdom-shaking. I have not fallen short. I have not missed the boat. And I am not a mistake. I am right where He needs me to be and I'm ready... Ready to chase His heart and follow His path for my life. I want to live fully alive! I want to dance! And I'm jumping fully in today!

I am healing and I am standing firm in my authority over the enemy.

I am no longer allowing the enemy to use my scars, my mistakes, and my past to keep me in a cycle of pain, shame, and anger. I serve the One True Healer and I know how much He loves me. There will be times when my old scars, my old battles, still try to call my name, but I am learning that I can lean into my Heavenly Father and He will help me rise above and give me the strength to overcome. And though my heart has seen days in the fetal position, He has always caught me in the fall, called me out of the hopelessness and lit my way; sometimes one tiny and painful step at a time, but always faithfully there. On the days when I feel the same familiar and tormenting pain begin to creep in, I know now that the enemy has no power over me and I am not a product of my feelings or my past. I am healing because He is healing me. And He will see me through. I will process and, at times I may still hurt, but I can give it to Him over and over, as many times as it takes. I am not forever broken, destined to stay in this same defeating cycle. He is my hope.

He is calling me, every day, to draw closer to Him.

He doesn't want or expect a blind love from me that seeks only to please a God that I don't know. He wants me to know Him... truly *know* Him. He wants me to hear His heart. To feel His love. And in knowing Him,

297

to delight in Him. To share my day with Him. And to share my heart with Him. To understand His unconditional and divine love and allow it to take root in my heart and give me rest, peace, hope and joy. The invitation reads simply and beautifully...

Draw close and truly know me. Seek to know me deeply and fully. Today. And every day. And watch as I completely transform your heart and your life. I will pour over you. I will heal you. I love you. You are mine.

To My Readers

We've made it, friends!

I want to first thank you for taking this journey with me. Chasing joy is not always easy and we have ventured together through some very deep and meaningful healing. I'm praying that you have experienced some truly powerful and life-changing breakthroughs. I'm praying that you are feeling joy and hope begin to pour into your spirit again. But mostly, I'm praying that this journey has helped you draw closer to the One True Healer, Jesus, and that you have felt His touch, and His presence, throughout.

I deeply appreciate your private moments of great vulnerability with me; the moments when you have cried with me, prayed with me, and walked through the really, really hard with me. And I appreciate your heart and your grace more than you know. Together, we have fully embraced this idea that joy is possible in even the most difficult seasons. We have been stretched, but we have grown as well.

Please don't let the process of healing, discovering, and growing end here. Keep seeking Him in all that you do! Keep watering your spirit and keep shining! You are absolutely incredible and unconditionally loved!

As always, blessings on your journey!

Shannon

To My Incredible Husband:

For a girl who always has plenty to say, words completely escape me when it comes to my deep appreciation and love for you. You are truly my best friend and one of my biggest blessings. This journey, this life of ours, is simply and beautifully made so much better because we get to share it with you.

I hope you always know how truly loved you are. I hope you always feel how much Ryan and I appreciate and admire you. I hope you can always see that I'm so incredibly proud of you and everything that you have overcome and become!

Twenty years ago, we started out as two kids, clueless about life but dreaming of adventures and growing old together. We've since grown into a beautiful family and journeyed through the easy and even some of the really hard. I couldn't be more grateful for this life with you! You complete us.

To My Family & Friends:

How can I begin to express my deep and heartfelt appreciation for your never-ending encouragement and support? I am truly blessed beyond measure. Thank you so much for sharing this journey with me! I love you *very much* and I carry you in my heart always! Know this... *I thank God for you* each and every day!

Humbly yours, Shannon

About the Author

SHANNON SINGH is the face and heart behind the blog, Raising a Blessing. Mostly she's just a simple small-town girl who feels a deep calling to love on people and share God's hope in the hard.

After an incredibly difficult season in her life, Shannon began to feel a calling on her heart to share her story as well. As she journeyed through healing and chasing joy and radically experienced God's outpouring in the storm, her writing became a true extension of her love for Jesus, her love for others, and a big piece of her ministry.

Shannon lives in the mountains with her little family. When she's not writing, she's homeschooling her little guy, teaching as an adjunct college instructor, crafting on her kitchen table, or hiking with her two favorite people and their little (big) lab, Obi.

You can personally connect with Shannon on one of her blog platforms: www.RaisingaBlessing.com
Facebook: facebook.com/RaisingaBlessing

Made in the USA
Columbia, SC
15 January 2023